Anchored In His Love

Copyright © 2008, 2015 by Sandi Borgens

ISBN 978-0-979799-3-8

You may contact author by email
anchored@swbell.net

Scripture taken from the New King James Version.
Copyright © 1979, 1980, 1982 by Thomas Nelson, Inc.
Used by permission. All rights reserved.

Contents may not be reproduced in whole or part without the written permission of the author.

Cover design by Keith and Donna Cherry

Printed in The United States of America. All rights reserved under International Copyright Law.

Dedication

Anita, Todd and Rodd,

I give all praise and thanks to God for allowing me to share my journey with you, my dearest children. You are answered prayers and God's most precious gift to me. Before you were born, God knew you and I prayed for you. You are steadfast and have always stayed close to me regardless of our perils, circumstances, and hardships.
Humbled by your love, understanding, and kindness,
I dedicate this book to you.

With all my love...now and forever,

Mother

Acknowledgements

Anchored In His Love could not have been published without the help, understanding and prayers that my good friend, Kathy H'Sell gave me.

My publisher, Donna Cherry tirelessly gave of herself to have this book in print. Through the guiding of the Holy Spirit and prayers, she made this book possible.

To each and every one of you who encouraged me to complete this project I want to say,

"Thank You".

Foreword

Bless the Lord, O my soul; And all that is within me, bless His holy name!
Psalm 103:1

Sandi Borgens is one of the kindest, sweetest, most childlike women I know. She is one of the most misunderstood women I know. Many mistake her childlike demeanor as childish but, quite the contrary, she is anything but that. She is acutally more mature than many of those who would demean her or set themselves above her. Why would I say that, because Jesus said we should be like little children, and such are the ones to whom the Kingdom of God belongs. You see in God's perspective she has reached a level of maturity that many of us will never attain. But then, that's how His Kingdom operates, quite the opposite of ours. In our system of things it wouldn't be wise to spend your retirement on feeding the poor, or clothing the naked. But God says, "lay up for yourselves treasures in heaven, where neither moth nor rust destroys and where thieves do not break in and steal" Matthew 6:20. We think maturity is being poised and dignified and that childlike faith or naivete in a grown person means they're immature or childish.

Anchored In His Love

Sandi Borgens, despite a life of rejection, tragedy upon tragedy, and hurt upon hurt has maintained a love for people and a faith combined with trust in mankind that many would have thrown out the window a long time ago. She has maintained a trust and belief that despite her cirucmstances God will see her through, uphold and protect her and strenghten her to ride any wave of adversity that will come her way. Not only will she go through the storm but she will remain loving, kind and sweet through it no matter how afraid she may be. She does it afraid until her faith overrides her fear. That's maturity. As you read the chapters of her life and see one event after another wherein any single one of them would have stopped most people or crippled them to some degree, you will see that Sandi has come through and each event has strengthened her faith, not diminished it. In the pages of this book you will find a woman who never lost faith, is enduring until the end, and while she's hanging on for dear life will throw a hand out to catch you to keep you from falling.

You'll find it hard to believe that all these events could happen to one person, but they did. Most will be amazed that she did not end up in a brothel, crack house or nut house, but I'm not. You see I know the God she knows and I encourage you to get to know Him too. Read her book and enjoy it. I did. Then if you don't already have a relationship with Jesus, I encourage you to pray and ask Him to come into your life and to be your Lord, Savior and Friend.

Donna Cherry
Waymaker Publishers

Table of Contents

Dedication	v
Acknowledgements	vii
Foreword	ix
Synopsis	xiii
In The Beginning	15
Legally Abandoned	21
A Real Home?	31
Divine Appointment	53
Caution Lane Change Ahead	59
Grandmother-Teacher-Friend	69
The Truth About Michael	75
Catastrophic Counsel	85
God's Greatest Gifts	89
Rewind And Start Again	103
The Mission	115
The Mysterious Letter	123
My Other Mother	129
Oh To Know My Mother	135
Never Ending Surprises	149
Epilogue	163

Synopsis

Trust in the Lord with all your heart, And lean not on your own understanding; In all your ways acknowledge Him, And He shall direct your paths.
Proverbs 3:5, 6

My goal in writing this book is to encourage people whose lives have been molded by experiences that have left them emotionally handicapped in one form or another. Maybe fears have gripped them, or heartbreak and loneliness. Many people suffer from rejection and don't know how to ever feel accepted. There is a way to feel whole again. I want them to know that there is a Heavenly Father that loves and watches over them. He will keep them through the darkest night and anchor them when there seems no solid ground to stand on during the storms of life that rage against them. We must remember it is not His will when these things happen but, the will of man, deceived by a liar and a thief, named Satan.

A person who does not submit their life to the will of

 *Anchored In His Love*

God but lives out their life according to their own desires will never truly find peace and happiness. Equally so, a person who will or does not allow God to guide them when hurts come their way will not know how to find healing. They will stumble through life wounded and will wound others. Just as a wounded animal attacks anyone or anything that comes near it as an act of protection, we too, lash out as a way of protecting ourselves. A cycle of being wounded and wounding others begins, and until someone gets healed it usually isn't broken. The healing power of God is the only answer.

To the degree we allow God to guide us, we will see a higher level of joy and happiness. He created us and all that is in the world. Just as a mechanic knows what your car needs to keep it running smoothly, so God knows how to keep us from falling apart along the rough roads we travel in life.

In The Beginning

Chapter 1

For Thou did form my inward parts; Thou didst weave me in my mother's womb.
Psalm 139:13

The beginning can only be told as it has been related to me in bits and pieces through the years as I've asked questions and dug deep to know the truth. My parents, Loretta Ann and Milton Dean (Mike), were married in 1937. A little over a year later, my brother, Michael was born. It seemed that while it wasn't necessarily in their plans to have a baby so soon, they adored him.

My mother apparently had always wanted a son and enjoyed watching Michael play and grow as most children do. To her dismay she found herself pregnant again and while abortions were not legal at that time she approached my father and asked him about getting one. He would have no part of it. He insisted that my mother keep the baby and so she did not have an abortion.

To all those with watching eyes at the hospital when I was born it must have appeared that we were quite the happy little family. I'm told my mother was everything but happy about having had another baby.

We all came home and things went back to normal for my father and my brother, Michael but, as for my mother, she had changed. Maybe it was postpartum depression or just plain depression but, she refused to have any part in caring for me. She resented me and would leave me lay in a dark corner, crying and hungry. She wouldn't touch me even to change my diapers unless someone was visiting or my father was due to come home. If a visitor tried to hold me or care for me, she would simply say that she didn't want me to get spoiled and leave me to cry.

On the other hand, when my father came home he would take me outside, play with me and pay attention to me. This infuriated my mother.

My mother resented the attention my father paid to me. This was attention she would have received if I had not been born and she had been allowed to have an abortion. She had a son, that's all she had wanted but now she had not just another baby, she had a girl! To make matters worse my father, according to all I've been told, seemed to adore me and that's not what my

 *In The Beginning*

mother wanted—she wanted to be adored! Needing attention, she would soon find it another way.

One day when my father was at work she left Michael, who was still not quite two years old and me, a tiny infant, at home alone. She had gone to meet and be with another man, someone with whom she was the focus, and she liked that. Now, Michael wasn't really old enough to care for himself, much less me but, she didn't really care. Her unfounded, unnatural jealousy of me had blocked all reason from her mind. Perhaps if this had happened today she would have been treated for postpartum depression and all would have gone back to normal. But without understanding of how she felt, her reactions to a new baby and no treatment or medication, my mother slipped into a world she would never come out of.

My mother came back home that evening before my father got home from work and he was none the wiser. She began to go out regularly after that. As so often happens, she must have gotten careless because only a short time went by before my father found out what she had been doing. When I was about nine months old he had been gone several days in a row for work related reasons, and when he returned home unexpectedly, he discovered what his wife had been doing. Apparently she had left us alone for those several days that she knew he wouldn't be home at all. The condition he found us in was deplorable. Poor little Michael had done his best to care for me. When

 *Anchored In His Love*

our father found him, Michael was trying to feed and comfort me. I had not had my diaper changed in days and my curly hair was all matted. My father was about to leave and take us to his mother's when our mother returned and saw what he was planning to do. She refused to let him take Michael, so he grabbed me and went to my grandmother's.

When he got to my grandmother's home, my dad's sister and her children were there. Not wanting her children to see the deplorable condition I was in they were sent into another room.

When they tried to take my diaper off it stuck to my skin but, even more horrifying was what came crawling out of my diaper—maggots! They placed me in a sink of warm water to let the diaper soak. This made removing it easier. They did not want to hurt the tender, raw skin of my soft, little baby bottom. When the diaper could finally be removed they discovered I had ringworm from having worn the foul diaper for so long.

My father had made the decision that he could no longer stand by and tolerate my mother's behavior. The combination of her running around with other men, and leaving my brother and me on our own contributed to the break up of their marriage. Just a short five months later, when I was around fourteen months old and Michael was a little over two years old, our parents got a divorce.

Needless to say there was a custody battle. Our

 *In The Beginning*

mother tried to get custody of both of us because that was the only way she could get Michael. Of course her actions had been taken into consideration and when the decision was made as to who would have custody, it was granted to our father. The judge knew he had been the one who, upon finding out what our mother had been doing, rearranged his life to care for us and keep us safe.

> *Even more horrifying was what came crawling out of my diaper—maggots!*

Our dad loved us very much and was glad he had won custody but, he now had a dilemma. What would he do with us while he worked? Jobs were scarce, the Great Depression and World War II were still having an affect on the economy. If you had a job you wanted to keep it. My father worked long hours as a red cap, checking bags at the airport and couldn't miss any more work to care for us. He went to his mother and asked if she would help him by keeping us during the day but, she was ill. She wanted to help but, her health prevented it. She had been in and out of the hospital because her gallbladder had ruptured causing infection to spread throughout her body. This had weakened her physically and the doctors had advised her not to take on the responsibility of raising two small children.

My father turned to his sister and brother-in-law next.

 *Anchored In His Love*

He knew they loved the us very much and hoped they would help. To his dismay they not only wanted to take us, they wanted to adopt us as their own. They were afraid they would become even more attached and then lose us if our father's circumstances changed.

Our father did the only thing in his mind he could do until his circumstances changed; he put us in a Christian based children's home until he could work something else out. At least that was his plan...

Legally Abandoned

Chapter 2

*When my father and my mother forsake me,
Then the Lord will take care of me.*
Psalm 27:10

When I was only about fifteen months old and Michael was almost three, we entered the children's home. Neither one of us really understood what was happening to us or realized the dramatic turn our lives had just taken. Our parents were gone. While our mother had not been the best mother and our father spent long hours working, children love and need their parents. Michael was frightened and lost, and I was really too young to sense anything except the loss of familiar surroundings. We had gone from one circumstance of neglect to a different circumstance of neglect.

Anchored In His Love

During the next six years, we did not receive the nurturing love and attention that most children come to expect from their mothers and fathers. Remember Michael was loved by both our parents and I had the love and attention of my father. He had at least been nurturing when he was home. He played with me, took me outside and tended to my needs and even as a baby, I'm sure I sensed his love and knew his voice and touch. Instead, we had impersonal caregivers with the job of making sure we, and all the other children at the home, followed and obeyed all the rules of the home.

Because I was so young when we first entered the home, my memories of this time are limited. The only person that stands out in my mind is Ms. Brown, an older lady who took care of the younger girls at the home. I remember Ms. Brown because she had a nice smile and didn't cause me any harm.

The first vivid memories I have of the children's home centered on my bed-wetting. When I was about three or four years old, many times after getting into bed for the night, I would have to go to the bathroom. My bed was more of a large crib with high rails and it involved climbing over the top of the rails to get out of it. Not only did I have to overcome this obstacle but, there was no night light. While the room was a large dormitory room with beds all lined up in a row and there were other little girls in the room, there were no adults nearby if someone needed assistance. The bathroom was down an unlit hall and fear of the dark made it even more difficult for me to get out of bed to go to the bathroom. I was terribly afraid that something was lurking in the dark, ready to pounce on me. The thought of walking alone across the cold floor, in the dark by myself, was just too overwhelming. I would try asking one of the other girls in the room to go with me but, many times no one wanted to, I suppose they were tired or wanted to stay in their warm beds.

When I couldn't find anyone to go with me to the bathroom, paralyzed by my fear I would wet my bed! Unfortunately, this always resulted in a spanking. Bed-wetting was not tolerated at the home. Now this spanking was often times a most unusual spanking. First, a warning was given, after that you were given a regular spanking, and finally it was...the spanking machine! Yes, a spanking machine. There were paddles that rotated around in a circle and continuously paddled the bottom of some poor frightened little child like myself, as each paddle made the circle.

> *First you were given a warning, then a regular spanking, and finally it was...the spanking machine!*

Boys and girls were separated at meal times, and slept in separate dormitories. We both came to the home at such young ages neither of us remembered

 *Anchored In His Love*

we had a brother or a sister. The home made no effort to ensure that we were aware of each other as brother and sister or that we interacted as such. Why I don't know, they just didn't.

At meal times boys and girls sat at different tables. I remember noticing a frail looking little boy who often would sit at his table looking sad or crying and I would tell my friends sitting at my table that when I grew up I was going to marry that little boy. Little did I know that the little boy I intended to marry was really my brother.

When I was five years old meal times had become a terrible ordeal. In the mornings they would serve cold oatmeal and liver! Can you imagine, liver is hard enough to stomach for dinner but with oatmeal for breakfast! Then to make matters worse, much of the meat served at the other meals was very fatty, and every time I ate it, I would get an upset stomach and vomit.

I knew I would be punished if I didn't clean my plate at every meal, so I would try to give the fatty meat to a friend sitting next to me at the table or drop it onto the floor. Now this was risky because if the caregivers saw me do this I would be punished. More often than not I would get physically sick and throw up during meal times. This resulted in me being placed on a chair in the hall all alone waiting for someone to take me to the hospital that was next door to the home. During these times I remember feeling very sad and scared as I sat there all alone and waited.

 *Legally Abandoned*

At Christmas time our father would send presents for Michael and me but, we never received them. It wasn't until years later that I learned he had sent gifts and had also sent candy and fruit. Unfortunately what our father had meant for us was instead kept and eaten by the director of the home.

There are two events that stand out in my memory about this time in my life. These same two events were also captured in the only photographs I have of myself before the age of six. The first photograph is a picture taken of me sitting on a small rocking horse when I was about three years old. In this photo I'm clutching a small stuffed panda bear, and I have a sad, worried look on my face. The home used this photo on the cover of one of their brochures to promote the Children's Home. Two additional photos captured the second event that was also associated with the children's home. When I was about five years old I was chosen to play the part of the bride in a "Tom Thumb" mock wedding that the children's home put together. I'm not certain why this event took place, and I have never heard of anything like it since but, I remember how happy I was all dressed up in the pretty white gown, and walking down the aisle of a church. I loved being in church. Even now, I remember the feelings of love and peace I experienced when I was in church.

The following pages contain photographs of me on the rocking horse and the Tom Thumb wedding. In

Anchored In His Love

Legally Abandoned

Tom Thumb Wedding Photos

the photograph of me being escorted down the aisle, take note of the man in a suit and tie sitting to my left. I was told years after I had grown up that this man had wanted to adopt me but, had not been allowed to because he had wanted to only adopt me, and not my brother as well. Also, notice in this picture that I was intently looking at an elderly lady to my right. This was Ms. Brown. She was the closest thing to a mother image I had and like any other young child, I looked for the face I could trust. Ms. Brown was the caregiver for the younger girls at the home.

The second photograph is also of the mock wedding but, this one shows the whole "wedding party". When you look at the picture, notice I am not smiling in this picture either. Again, I'm intently looking at someone off camera, at Ms. Brown.

The only home I had ever known was the orphanage. My entire life up to this point, that I could remember, included only the orphanage, the children in it and the people associated with it. I didn't know who I was or anything about why I was there. There would be times at church when I would see children with their mothers and fathers and it was only natural that I yearned for my own parents. I didn't know where they were or why I didn't live with them. No one had ever explained to me the circumstances of why I was at the orphanage.

I had no idea what a real home was like, or what it would feel like to have a family but, I desperately wanted someone to love and to be loved in return. I remember many times crying when I saw those children with their parents in church and wondered how it must be to have parents to love you or what it meant to be in a family with brothers and sisters instead of other children with no parents.

> *I didn't know who I was or anything about why I was there.*

During the six years Michael and I spent at the orphanage there were different occasions when I would spend a couple of weeks in the summer with a family that was associated with the orphanage. This gave me a glimpse of what it might be like in a real home but, because I was a guest and treated like a guest and not like a family member, I really didn't know what it would be like to have or be in a real family.

The orphanage was a Christian based home and they taught us some fundamental truths about God and faith. They taught us that God was our Heavenly Father, and with no earthly father that I knew of, this sounded great to me. We were taught about prayer and that we could talk to God anytime we wanted. Well, if He was my Heavenly Father then I certainly grabbed on to that and talked to Him often. I once asked Him the question I couldn't bring myself to ask anyone else, "What is it like to live in a real home?"

 Anchored In His Love

In a way I didn't expect He would soon show me the answer to that question.

    I found peace and comfort in my times of prayer and I know now it's because He's real and His presence is tangible. When we talk to Him, He comes in a tangible way for us to experience Him and the Bible tells us that *in His presence is fullness of joy*. He came and His presence got me through very difficult times. His presence has continued to get me through tough times throughout my life.

    From time to time, an elderly couple would come to the home. They would wait patiently in the front hall for the director to bring me and Michael down so they could visit with us. I recognized the little boy as the boy I wanted to marry when I grew up. Although this couple was virtually strangers to both of us, Michael and I were encouraged to call them "Grandma and Grandpa". Sometimes they would bring us gum or candy. Sounds nice doesn't it but, we were not allowed to keep these gifts because the home wouldn't allow it. If our grandparents were caught giving the candy and gum to us, or worse yet, if we ate the candy or chewed the gum, we were forced to give it back or spit it out right there in front of them.

    This ultimately began to wear on our grandfather and a change would soon be made.

A Real Home?

Chapter 3

*"This is the day which the Lord has made;
Let us rejoice and be glad in it."*
Psalm 118:24

I clearly remember the day, when I was six and a half years old, that Ms. Brown told me I would be leaving the children's home and going to a real home. I had wondered what a real home would be like and now I was going to find out, and I was scared! All I had ever known in my life was the children's home; I really couldn't imagine anything else.

As I said before, through the years at the orphanage, I had spent some time in real homes for a few weeks over the summer months with a family who was connected to the children's home in some way or another but, I never got to stay more then a few weeks.

 Anchored In His Love

I was always sent back to live at the children's home.

Now, here I was leaving the children's home for good, and going to a real home of my own. You can imagine, I was filled with mixed emotions. As I pulled my personal belongings and the few toys I owned from the little cubby hole assigned to me, and then hugged the other little girls goodbye, fear of the unknown and sadness were only two of the many emotions that I was feeling. I was leaving the only life I had ever known. Curiosity, at what new things would be in store for me, was another of those emotions going through my mind. Seems like a lot for one little six year old to absorb doesn't it—it was. Then before I knew it... it was time to go.

> *I was filled with mixed emotions... I was leaving the only life I had ever known.*

I was surprised to discover the couple I had been instructed to call Grandma and Grandpa waiting for me in the lobby. However, they weren't the only ones waiting there. The little boy named Michael was there too. They were there to take both me and Michael home with them. I still had no idea this little boy was really my older brother and that this elderly couple were my paternal grandparents.

As we left the home, I turned and took one final

A Real Home?

look up the stairs to the large door that led into the home. I would not see this place again for many years.

My grandmother's health had improved some at this point. It was determined that she would be better able now to care for her two grandchildren, who were no longer infants, and have us come to live with them. The main contributing factor, for Michael and me going to live with them though, was really our grandfather. He could no longer bear to see how we were treated at the home and felt that our grandmother could handle us now that we were older. So, together the four of us rode the city bus to our grandmother and grandfather's home. When we got off the bus we walked less than a half block and turned up the walkway to a house with steps and a big porch. The house was close to an elementary school, and a hospital that had a nursing school attached to it. The nursing school backed up to our grandparents backyard and was separated by the fence.

Life had taken a dramatic turn for me. I was now living with my real grandparents but, to me they were essentially strangers. Yes, I was acquainted with them but nonetheless they were still only slight acquaintances who at times had visited Michael and me and had tried to bring us candy. This time I was old enough to understand that my life had just taken a dramatic change. Everything I had ever known or could remember was back at the children's home.

While there had been many strict rules and

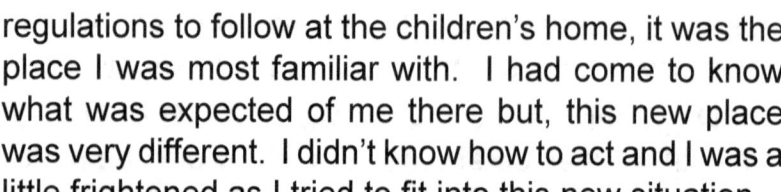

regulations to follow at the children's home, it was the place I was most familiar with. I had come to know what was expected of me there but, this new place was very different. I didn't know how to act and I was a little frightened as I tried to fit into this new situation.

The first rule I quickly learned was that children were to be seen and not heard. Being located near a hospital zone made it convenient for Grandma and Grandpa to rent out the upstairs to nurses and the occupational and physical therapy students from the nearby hospital and medical school. This supplemented their small income. Loud noises of any kind were frowned upon.

Even though our grandparents had opened their home to us, they expected us to adapt to the rules of the house. Few changes were made to accommodate the fact that there were now two children under the age of eight years old living in their house.

We had gone from one set of strict rules to a different set of rules. While we were now being cared for by our grandparents and not employees of an orphanage, we still did not receive any real nurturing. There was no tender, gentle loving arms to hold and caress us or the sweet words of encouragement to succeed at a task too large for us. We didn't hear words like "honey" or "sweetie" that so many grandparents use today. Can you imagine being a small child and never hearing words like that spoken to you in soft cooing voices but, more importantly yet, never being told that you

A Real Home?

were loved? I never heard someone say to me, "I love you" until I was an adult. This was such a powerful thing to hear, so much so that on the day someone did say it I had to ask them to repeat it because it was so incredible to me.

> *I never heard someone say to me, "I love you" until I was an adult.*

There was one other thing that wasn't too different about living at my grandparents house—going to the bathroom, this was still an ordeal for me.

There was no bathroom on the first floor. The bathroom was in the basement and there wasn't a light in the room after you closed the door for privacy. I was still afraid of the dark, which is not so unusual for a lot of six year olds. After some time my grandmother accommodated me by giving me something to use at night so I wouldn't have to go down in the dark basement all by myself. Yet even in the daytime, the thought of closing that door and sitting in the dark was still terrifying. I hate to admit it but, even today when I face going into dark areas I pray.

It was difficult being quiet all the time. Children play, get excited, laugh, and just make noise doing ordinary things. I quickly learned that even singing, something that always made me happy, was now something I would no longer be able to do living in my

 *Anchored In His Love*

grandparents home.

Since all the upstairs rooms were being used by the boarders, Michael and I didn't even have our own bed, or bedroom. Together, we slept in the living room. Michael slept on the couch, while I slept on a chair that made into a bed. Although Grandma's health was better, she would be so tired at the end of the day from cleaning her house and the rented rooms, that Michael and I quickly learned to put ourselves to bed each evening.

When we first arrived at our grandparents home the two biggest surprises for me was being told that our grandparents were our real grandparents, (except Grandpa, he was our step-grandfather) and that Michael was my real brother! All this time in the home watching him be sad and cry, thinking I would marry him someday and then to hear he was my brother was incredible to me. While we had been told the truth about each other and our grandparents, nothing was mentioned about our parents and we didn't ask—why I don't remember or it just didn't occur to us I guess.

As we settled into our new home and life at our grandparents, we grew close and turned to each other for companionship. There weren't many children in our neighborhood and for the first time in our lives we were allowed to play together. Before long we were doing everything together. Michael became my best friend.

A favorite game that Michael and I loved to play

A Real Home?

together was cowboys in the backyard. Before too long we settled into this new life with our grandparents.

A picture of us taken not too long after we went to live with our grandparents, shows us dressed in our Sunday best. You see Michael, a boy small for his age and me smiling shyly for the camera with long curly hair and a big bow. We kept growing closer and Michael and I protected each other. We never had an argument.

One day when I was about eight years old, and Michael was still nine, our Grandpa took us to the park to play with a new boat that Michael had just built. We were both excited about this new adventure. I remember being very proud of Michael.

After Michael put the boat in the water, a big wind came and took the boat to the middle of the lake. We weren't able to get the boat back. Standing and watching the boat that was out of our reach, we hugged each other and cried.

Even though I had discovered my brother, and was now living with my real grandparents, it was still a lonely life. Michael had started playing with one of the few neighborhood boys, and the little boy didn't like me playing with them. Grandma was busy taking care of the house and her boarders and Grandpa was not the type of Grandpa a little girl could play with, so this left me to play alone for hours. I played with paper dolls. Like many girls do, I played house with my paper dolls but, in my case, I pretended they were

 A Real Home?

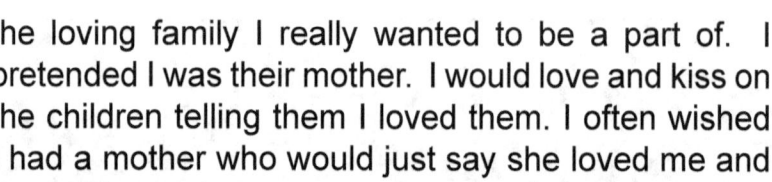

Anchored In His Love

the loving family I really wanted to be a part of. I pretended I was their mother. I would love and kiss on the children telling them I loved them. I often wished I had a mother who would just say she loved me and would kiss me! A mother who would play house and dolls with me like the other children I knew.

Being surrounded by older people, I didn't grow up like normal children. Since I was alone most of the time, and no one really communicated with me because they were busy working or sleeping, I became shy and withdrawn. Don't misunderstand me, while I was shy and not an out going person I loved to be around people and still do. Then and now it takes me a while to open up to people and talking with strangers is not something I'm comfortable with. However, around people I know and family, it's different. I enjoy talking and laughing and having a good time as most people do. Having no one to talk with or play with was very hard for me. I've discovered as an adult that I still don't like being alone.

Going to school was something I looked forward to and thoroughly enjoyed. This was a time when I could interact with kids my own age. I could play, sing, run and do what children do. I grew to hate summer vacation because I wasn't able to see my friends for that three month period. I would cry the last day of school knowing it would be three months before I would play with other children again.

When I was eight years old I became a majorette

A Real Home?

at my school. I would twirl my baton for hours in the backyard, discovering that it helped to pass the time. Practicing to twirl my baton would fill my days. I had nothing else to do and so I found myself becoming quite good at baton twirling. This gave me comfort in some way.

I prayed every night that God would give me a baby sister. Once I even told my Grandma that I wanted a baby sister for Christmas. My Grandma told me to talk to my father. You see, finally at this point, we had been reintroduced to our father—somewhat. While we had not been told immediately when we moved in with our grandparents that our father was alive they did eventually tell us about him. Take note here, they told us about our father, not a word about our mother. When they first told us about him it was only information but, after a period of time we had minimal contact with him.

When I was allowed to, I would call him on the phone. We shared a line with other people in our area known as a party-line in those days. I remember thinking of him as a "telephone daddy". The real treat was when he came at Christmas to visit us and bring presents. His visits were always brief. Sometimes he didn't even stay to visit when he brought the presents. On those occasions we were told Santa brought the presents. Eventually they told us the truth that he had brought the presents but couldn't stay. I think our grandparents knew that we would be hurt if we found out that he had come over and didn't visit with us. The excuse they always gave us was that he had to work.

I was somewhere around the age of eleven years old when our father bought a delicatessen. It was about this same time our grandfather had passed away and Grandma no longer had his social security income. Our father would bring food and supplies to supplement the small amount of groceries our grandmother could then afford due to her decrease in income. Our father hadn't helped with our expenses much up to this point. Our grandfather, as I had said earlier, was only our step-grandfather making him our father's stepdad. For what reasons I don't know but, while our Grandpa was alive our father did not visit much or help out financially. After Grandpa's death he did visit and call more, not often, just more often, and he helped our grandmother a little financially by

> *I would call him on the phone when I was allowed to...I remember thinking of him as a "telephone daddy".*

providing the food and supplies.

Before Grandpa died I remember feeling that he had been the kindest to me. I enjoyed being around him. He would take time on occasion to treat us like kids and do things with us, like the time he took us to the park with Michael's boat. He had helped Michael make

A Real Home?

the boat and they had a good time together making it.

Unfortunately, he developed Alzheimer's Disease and had to go to a state hospital and remained there until he died. They didn't call it Alzheimer's then but, now I know that's what it was. Before he was sent to the hospital and we had discovered that he wasn't behaving normally, he would say really mean things. This was unusual and for some reason, it seemed he wanted to be the meanest to me. I didn't understand it at that time, and it hurt me terribly. He had always been so kind to me. He would blame me for things that I didn't do and I would be disciplined for things unjustly.

I know now why he did these things but, then it was just one more thing to add to my pain and loneliness. Eventually when he got worse and began forgetting who people were and saying strange things, people began to think he was losing his mind from old age. That's when it was decided he would go to the state hospital. In my child mind it was just one more case of someone I loved being removed from my life again.

My grandparents had tried very hard to take care of us while Grandpa was alive. After Grandpa died, Grandma still did her best to provide for us on her limited income. She was sickly and went to the doctor all the time but, nonetheless, she made sure we had the things we needed. Everything went well for about three years, until Grandma got sick enough to go to the hospital. While she was in the hospital, a distant relative of Grandpa's came and took care of us. She was very stern and quite fearsome.

Both Michael and I hoped Grandma would get well soon and worried what would happen to us if she didn't. While we were acquainted with our father we weren't quite sure that he would be the one who would take care of us. After all, we were living with our grandparents and not him. Much to our relief, Grandma did recover and was well enough to come home from the hospital but, her health was always very precarious.

It was a bittersweet thing when our grandfather died because as I said before, our father called more after Grandpa died. He still didn't spend the time with us the way a father should though. The only time I remember my father taking me anywhere was when we attended a Girl Scout father/daughter banquet together. Grandma had begged him to take me, and finally he said yes. I was thrilled and scared all at the same time. I was excited about finally getting to spend some time alone with my father but, I was also scared because he was really a stranger to me. When I got into the car I found that I didn't know what to say to him. I was very shy and quiet on the ride to the banquet and he didn't do much to draw me out either, I guess he felt a little awkward too.

The evening didn't really turn out as I hoped it would. Although we went to the banquet, after the meal was over my father asked another father there if he would drive me home. I was so upset that he wasn't taking me home and began to cry, which only

 *A Real Home?*

angered my father somewhat. He said he had to get back to work but, I later discovered this wasn't the truth. Many years later it was told to me that my father attended the horse races each night. I learned that many of the times we were told he was working he was really going to the races. I'm glad I didn't know this until I was old enough to handle it. God in His mercy kept many hurtful things from me until I was better able to understand them and cope with them.

Remember I had told my grandmother I wanted a baby sister, and I had been praying for one. I went so far as to make a place for her next to me on my chair bed at night so God could deposit her beside me while I slept. I would like to say at this time that God answers our prayers. Sometimes He answers in ways we don't understand and at times in ways we are unaware of. God always has a plan and a purpose, and His plans are always for our good. When He doesn't answer prayers or answers in a way we don't understand or even know that He's answered, we have to trust despite what we see. The Bible says in Romans 8:28, *"And we know that all things work together for good to those who love God, to those who are called according to His purpose"*. What does that mean, called according to His purpose? It means when we love Him and yield to His plan for our life, what He has purposed and called us to, He will work **all** things out for our good. I would later in life find this to be true when I discovered unanswered prayers were indeed answered, only not as I had thought they would be.

Anchored In His Love

After a few years of praying for this baby sister and none came, I decided to invent an imaginary friend. So, at meal times I would divide the food on my plate in half to share with my imaginary friend and my Grandma, not knowing about my imaginary friend would ask me why I was doing such an odd thing. Finally one day I told her and in her matter-of-fact and that's how it needs to be manner, she simply said, "Oh...well then—quit it." It didn't occur to her that I may have done this out of loneliness or some other emotional need, she simply said, "quit it." So, I quit it. Now, I didn't even have an imaginary friend. Loneliness had become an unwelcome friend. I knew it all too well.

For a time, I had a cat named Casey. I loved Casey. You see I could hold him, hug him and love on him and that satisfied a need for love in my life. To this day I am a cat lover. Casey was in reality, a stray cat that my grandmother had told me I could keep.

Unknown to me at that time, it seems some of the nuns in the area thought Casey was their cat too. I'm sure they didn't call him Casey because they didn't know about me and my claims on him, so they probably had their own name for him. Poor Casey! It's a good thing cats don't necessarily come when called by name isn't it! During the day Casey would go to their house but, at night I would bring Casey in and keep him with me.

One time Casey went missing for a few days and I inquired around the neighborhood asking the neighbors

A Real Home?

if they had seen him only to find out he had been injured and the doctors at the hospital had attended to him thinking he belonged to the nuns. I was glad they had attended to him, and because of my inquiry and concern everyone then realized that Casey was really my cat. Casey was my first pet and although I love all animals, I especially love cats. I presently have two pet cats. Just as I love all animals it seems they like me too. It could be because I enjoy taking little treats to my friends' pets when I visit their homes.

Going to school was still a place of socializing for me because I got to be with other children my age. As the years went by and I got older, I remember the other children making fun of me. They taunted me, asking me, *"What was wrong with you?"* or they would ask, *"Did you do something bad to make your parents leave?"*. Today we recognize that children can be knowingly and sometimes unknowingly cruel but, when I was a girl adults did not pay as much attention to the things that children said to one another and didn't take them as serious as we do today. We understand today that the things people say to us, even as children, can impact us well into our adult lives. Many young teenagers or children commit suicide today because of the cruel things that are said to them by their peers.

The children at school also made fun of the way I dressed. Grandma would buy my dresses a couple of sizes too large for me. A practical answer to a limited income yes but, this only made me stand out all the more. My red hair was extremely curly and hard to manage. I didn't have the right tools or accessories to tame it, and even if I had, I hadn't been taught by anyone how to comb thick, curly hair much less style it! My grandmother was busy with her boarders and caring for the house, so combing hair must have seemed a simple thing to her and she left me to do my own hair. If not having parents, or wearing clothes too big for me, and red unruly hair wasn't enough, to add to my embarrassment many times I would have to wear my brother's underwear!

I did think it a special treat when Aunt Dorothy, my father's sister and her husband, Uncle Lee would visit. They lived on a farm so they had to come late in the evening after the cows had been milked. They brought their three little daughters and I loved them dearly. I was so excited whenever they came for a visit. Seeing this happy family together always made me long to have my parents together and for us to be a family. Even though I had never met my mother to my knowledge, I knew I had to have had a mother and that my parents at one time had been together long enough to have two children. So, watching my aunt and uncle's family only increased that desire in me. Perhaps this is also where the desire for a baby sister came from. After all, these little girls had each other and always had someone to play with.

This was the same aunt and uncle who had wanted to adopt us when we were babies. While I could

A Real Home?

wonder what life would have been like if they had been allowed to adopt us, I have to remember what I said earlier about Romans 8:28 about working all things for my good. So while my life may seem to have been difficult and lonely God has taken it and turned it to my good, allowing me to have the children and husband I have today. I also have the loving testimony of what He has done in my life as a result. The Bible also says *"He will give us beauty for ashes"* (Isaiah 61:3).

> *To add to my embarrassment many times I would have to wear my brother's underwear!*

Another part of life at our grandparents included Grandma's friend, Helen who lived with her aging mother and her five other siblings. Imagine, six siblings all grown and not married still living together and taking care of their mother! They would often have Michael and me over on Sunday afternoons to give Grandma a break. I enjoyed spending time with Helen. She was like a big sister, or mother figure to me. Helen was the one who had introduced me to the paper dolls that I played with to occupy my time when Michael was playing with the little boy in our neighborhood. She subscribed to McCall's magazine and each month there were paper doll cutouts in it. She would let me cut out the dolls and the little clothing cutouts that were also included that month. She taught me to paste the dolls to cardboard and how to change their clothes and play with the dolls. While Helen had taught me these things it still was not like a mother showing love to her daughter. She was simply being kind and helping my grandmother. I appreciate the kindness she showed me and the things she taught me.

At Christmas, Helen and her siblings would take me and Michael to their house and give us a present. Sometimes this was a ploy to get us out of the house because our father was going to drop presents off at Grandma's and not stay to visit for Christmas. They knew we would be upset and disappointed and our father didn't want to deal with our reaction.

Despite these friendly neighbors, for me Christmas time was not like it was for my friends at school. It was still a lonely time, we didn't have lots of family and friends who came to visit or that we went to visit, and there wasn't a lot of presents. One year I got no presents at all. It seems I had disobeyed or done some minor thing wrong and the punishment for this offense was that I didn't receive a Christmas present. This offense happened very close to Christmas making it a *just* punishment I suppose. (This may have been one of the times Grandpa had blamed me when he was sick and we didn't know it. I don't remember all the details of it only that I didn't get a present).

Michael still received a present and something in his stocking. I got nothing in my stocking. I was crushed but, it didn't stop me from celebrating the birth

A Real Home?

of Jesus. I found some little something and made a present for Jesus for His birthday!

A few years went by and for the most part, my life had settled into a comfortable routine. I had adjusted to my life at my grandparents. There were times when I was sad and lonely that I would think about the children back at the children's home. I would wonder what they were doing, and I wanted to be with them.

During other times of sadness and loneliness I would stand for hours gazing out the back door of my Grandma's house dreaming about having a mother and a father to live with. I would ache for the love of my father who wasn't a real part of my life. I still prayed and talked with my Heavenly Father who remained very real to me but, I would think about how much I missed my dad, and wanted him to be part of my life. Still I was thankful for the teaching and realization that I had a Heavenly Father who did care.

When you're just a kid, you still ache for a tangible parent but, I can say that knowing and loving God was such a part of my life that **without that relationship I would not have survived**. I thank God that He didn't stop drawing me *even closer* to Him. I hungered to know more about Him and the opportunity would soon present itself. The healing found in His word, the Bible, would begin to change me.

Divine Appointment

Chapter 4

But those who wait on the Lord shall renew their strength; They shall mount up with wings like eagles, They shall run and not be weary, They shall walk and not faint.
Isaiah 40:31

For such a long time, I had wanted a friend so badly but, no friend ever came. By the time I was ten years old, the loneliness I felt had become a heavy burden I carried with me everywhere, and I desperately wanted to somehow escape the sad feelings that consumed me. It was at about this time in my life that I met Thelma.

Thelma was the youth teacher at the Presbyterian church I had started attending. She quickly became a special person in my life. Although this sweet lady was in charge of a group of children, I felt an immediate connection with her. She would drive me home after church so I wouldn't have to walk alone after dark.

Anchored In His Love

Thelma gave me the encouragement and attention I so desperately needed at this time in my life. For all of my young life, no one had really taken the time to tell me they loved me or tell me they thought I was special. So when Thelma would affectionately call me *"her brat,"* this meant the world to me. I saw it as a term of endearment that meant Thelma loved and cared for me. Little did either of us know at that time but, a lifelong friendship had begun. Throughout my life, no matter what was happening, Thelma would always be a part of it.

Going to church was such a special time for me. In addition to being with other children my age, I got the opportunity to sing again. Singing had always brought me such joy. I loved hearing all the hymns and being able to sing out loud once again was rejuvenating and invigorating to me. I might have been young but, my spirit had become so dull and now I was feeling alive again. Can you imagine having something in your life that could bring so much joy? Worshipping God and singing songs to Him did that for me.

One of the hymns I discovered at church was <u>Open My Eyes</u>, by Clara H. Scott. The words of this hymn, written in 1895, touched my heart in a way that none of the other hymns did. Throughout my life, this particular hymn has become a sort of anthem that I find myself humming or singing because the words minister to me in such a powerful, personal way.

 *Divine Appointment*

Open My Eyes
Clara H. Scott

Open my eyes, that I may see
glimpses of truth Thou hast for me;
place in my hands the wonderful key
that shall unclasp and set me free.
Silently now I wait for Thee,
ready, my God, Thy will to see.
Open my eyes, illumine me, Spirit divine!

Open my ears, that I may hear
voices of truth Thou sendest clear;
and while the wave notes fall on my ear,
everything false will disappear.
Silently now I wait for Thee,
ready, my God, Thy will to see.
Open my ears, illumine me, Spirit divine!

Open my mouth, and let me bear
gladly the warm truth everywhere;
open my heart and let me prepare
love with Thy children thus to share.
Silently now I wait for Thee,
ready, my God, Thy will to see.
Open my heart, illumine me, Spirit divine!

 *Anchored In His Love*

In addition to enjoying all the music, as part of the youth group, I was required to memorize about forty scriptures. I loved this! Imagine being able to read and memorize parts of the Bible. I always loved church but this was going to a new level for me. It was during this time, that by making a public declaration of asking Jesus into my heart and to be Lord of my life allowed me to get a Bible.

You must understand that as far back as I'm able to remember, Jesus always lived in my heart and I considered Him God and King. I had heard about Jesus at the orphanage and instantly it hit my little spirit and I asked Jesus *long ago* to be my Lord. But now I was being told that if I did it publicly they would give me a Bible! This treasure seemed too good to be true. When I got that Bible it became everything to me. It was the only book I owned, and I would read it for hours at a time, cover to cover, and then start over again. As I read the scriptures I took everything I read literally.

One of the scriptures I read said that Jesus calls me friend! (John 15:14, 15) **I discovered the friend I was so desperately seeking, and He had been there all along**. I knew God as my Heavenly Father and I knew I could pray and talk to Him but to consider Him *friend*, well He became the only true friend I had. As I read my Bible over and over I learned that Jesus would never leave me nor forsake me. This too was precious to me because everyone else I had come to love except my grandmother and my brother had left in some way. Just like praying to my Heavenly Father I could talk or pray to my Friend Jesus anytime I wanted to.

Even though I had prayed all those years and loved God, I was learning that it was those prayers, and His constant presence that was keeping me together during all the lonely times. During the scarey times, during the times I desperately wanted to be loved— He was there and He was loving me in a way that only He could. My Bible made things make sense.

Even though on the outside it looked like nothing had changed, for me **everything** had changed. Reading my Bible was the beginning of me learning about the love, the character of God, and why things happen to innocent people. Learning this helped me get through the difficult times, and believe me, there were more difficult times to come.

Through it all God was ever watching and working behind the scenes to provide me with the people and tools I needed to succeed, despite the attempts of the unseen thief who was working *"to kill, steal and destroy"* my life through the circumstances that happened to me (John 10:10).

Caution Lane Change Ahead

Chapter 5

Many are the afflictions of the righteous, But the Lord delivers him out of them all.
Psalm 34:19

There were some very dramatic events that happened to me during my teen years that had a great impact on me and these events set the stage for more heartache in the coming years. Looking back, I am forever thankful that I always had Jesus in my life. Things that could have destroyed me in any number of ways had no victory over me. There was always an anchor to hold onto.

I may have experienced loneliness and sadness because of these circumstances but, so do people who have not experienced abandonment, rejection and a lack of nurturing. Even when we love God with all our hearts our flesh still fails us, our emotions run amuck, and besides I was still just a child. Through all this, it was His love that kept me holding on and believing. His love is a tangible force that can be felt. It wasn't until I met Thelma that I began to learn and understand it but, I somehow always sensed it. She taught me about His love through her words and her actions then later in life I would learn how to recognize His tangible presence whether alone or in a crowd.

During my early teenage years, there were a couple of major things that happened in my life that had an impact on me for a number of years. One of them was that I had experienced several instances of sexual assault by two different people who lived in my neighborhood. I was frightened and intimidated by them after that and even embarrassed, although I don't know why I was embarrassed.

My grandmother noticed that I had been acting a little peculiar and unusually uncomfortable in certain situations around these people whom she knew and trusted, so she questioned me about it. I told her what had happened, and I will say she took precautions to ensure that I would not be put in those compromising situations again. Unlike so many other people I've heard tell their story of how they were accused of lying or being the aggressor or the one who had enticed or encouraged such advances, my grandmother did not do either of those. Today young girls are encouraged to discuss this topic and to tell if someone does

Caution-Lane Change Ahead

something like that to them but, this was not so when I was young. I am very thankful that my grandmother believed me and made sure nothing could happen to me like that again. She felt she was protecting me by not going forward with the information and I understand why she felt that way. The effects of how these encounters made me feel did not go away for several years. Again, until I gained an understanding of what the Bible had to say about me, why things happen to innocent people and what God can and will do to bring healing in our lives, if we allow Him to, I **was affected by feelings of shame, guilt and fear.**

> *I had experienced several instances of sexual assault...I was frightened and intimidated by them.*

The other event that had an impact on my life took place when I was sixteen years old. I had to quit school so I could help my grandmother by going to work in an office. I earned $45 a week, of which I gave all of it to my grandmother. Additional income was needed to buy food and groceries. Not only were Michael and I older now and requiring more food and our clothing costs were higher but, our ages required us to each have our own bedrooms for privacy. This meant she could only rent one room out to a tenant. This reduced her monthly income and it had to be made up somewhere.

When Michael was about 21 years old he had met a young girl and ran off to get married. The girl was only sixteen or seventeen years old at that time. They had a child right away and it seemed that they were happy. My personal feelings were that Michael married the first girl he dated as his way to combat the loneliness we both felt. His absence around the house left a great void and I missed him terribly.

I'll never forget the day the fire department came to do one of their routine inspections of my grandmother's home. The Fire Marshal determined that the upstairs could no longer be rented out. Michael had moved out and his room was available but it still could not bring the income the upstairs had brought in. My grandmother had a dilemma on her hands and unknown to me, so did I. Grandma not only needed the room Michael had just moved out of...but mine as well. **She asked me to move out!**

I was terrified. I didn't know how to be on my own. I had begun dating a man from work, who was much older than me, and I shared my terrifying news with him and he offered me a solution...he asked me to marry him, so I did. This seemed like a good and logical solution. I cared for this man, and we had been dating and gotten along alright. I really didn't understand love or relationships too well given my childhood experiences with love—one that was basically void of any that could be detected as love. My grandparents took us in because they loved us

Caution-Lane Change Ahead

I know but, it was projected more like responsibility than love. So, as much as any young woman with no real understanding of love, I thought I loved him.

Looking back, as so many of us do, I realized now that I married him for security and out of fear of living on my own. That more than likely was projected in my day to day interaction with him. I did love him like I said but, probably more like a father figure. He had been married before and had four children between the ages of three and twelve.

My grandmother thought he was okay and didn't really object to the marriage but, my father told me I was marrying a *used* man. He felt this way because my husband had been married before. My father most likely also thought he was too old for me. Secretly he may have wanted me to experience life a little more or perhaps find a younger man to actually be *in love* with and marry.

Regardless of whether he was right or wrong for me, this man brought me a security I hadn't known before. We moved into a house, and for a while I enjoyed being a wife and playing house. It was fun fixing up our new home. I kept our home clean and learned to cook because, after all, isn't that what grown-ups did.

You notice I said I enjoyed playing house and I thought that was what grown-ups did. I really didn't see myself that way. My husband would tell me I was a grown-up and I wasn't playing pretend. I had a hard

 *Anchored In His Love*

time seeing myself as an adult but, in reality that is what I had instantly become when I got married. I was no different than young people today who throw themselves into adult situations and have to take on responsibilities that they are not ready to handle. Like fruit, life must be experienced at the right time of maturity to be sweet, otherwise it will only be hard and bitter.

Young people today try to taste all life has way too early thinking they are mature when really they are no more ready to taste the things of life than a baby is ready to eat a steak! To add to my new responsibilities I also had to continue to work full-time to help pay the child support my husband was required to pay for his children from his first marriage. Instant adulthood and unprepared!

Shortly after I had gotten married, I met a lady by the name of Jane. Jane quickly became a dear friend and is one of the people in my life that has been more like a sister than a friend. Little did we know back then that our friendship would span a lifetime but it has. There is nothing that she would not do for me or me for her. Jane is a soft spoken person and truly is a prayer warrior. She has prayed so much for me that she has probably worn out her knees.

Jane was a rock for me when times were crumbling and she has always been there for me. We watched our kids grow up and shared everything with each other.

We share our life's most intimate secrets with one

Caution-Lane Change Ahead

another and we always laugh together, cry together and just plain enjoy each other's company. She was by far the person I needed to come into my life when she did because little did I know the things that were in store for me that I would need a friend and a prayer partner and warrior like her interceding on my behalf.

Three short months into my marriage I noticed little differences in my husband. He had quickly grown tired of me, and started going out. Perhaps my immaturity and lack of skills as a wife or partner were wearing on him. He worked days, while I worked nights to make ends meet, so it was easy for him to cheat on me, and he did.

> *Like fruit, life must be experienced at the right time of maturity to be sweet, otherwise it will only be hard and bitter.*

My husband also had outbursts of anger. There were times when he would attack me, holding my hands behind my back with one hand, while putting his other hand around my throat. Although I was so scared and troubled by his behavior, I didn't want to leave him because that meant I would be alone again. I kept making decisions in life based on fear. I was so completely frightened of being alone that I would endure his outbursts and cheating.

 *Anchored In His Love*

Many times after one of his outbursts, my husband wouldn't even remember what he had done. Often times when he found out about it, he would feel badly. I probably didn't help the situation by not talking to him about our problems but, I was always afraid it might cause one of his "spells". I had hoped ignoring them would just make them go away. They did get better for a period of time and he was good to me and I truly did grow to love him as a husband. It was only much later in my marriage that I found out that he had done the same thing to his first wife.

When I was twenty-one and half years old, I gave birth to a beautiful baby girl that we named Anita. This little brown-eyed, curly haired bundle was the joy of my life, a gift from God. She was the child that I had prayed for so long ago, only better because she was my daughter, not a sister.

Being a mother made me so very happy. Although I didn't know how to change a diaper or take care of a baby, I was on a mission to be the best mother I possibly could. Despite the problems in my marriage, I poured my energies into being a good mother.

Five and half years after Anita was born, I became pregnant with our son Todd. This was something we both wanted. While he already had one son, my husband wanted another one and I was glad because I wanted to have a son. But, to our surprise a little over two years later we had another son we named Rodd. My husband was not happy this time about the baby.

Considering his age at that time and that this made seven children for him, you can certainly understand how he felt. I'm sure it didn't help that I was thrilled!

Despite growing up without a mother of my own, I made the decision to be everything that I had ever wanted my own mother to be. I was a very "hands on" mother, who was always there for my children whenever they needed me. I wanted my children to feel the love and protection I had never known, and strived to teach them early about God and how much He loved them too.

During the difficult years of my marriage, the one blessing that came out of it was my children. Although I was fearful of my husband and his outbursts, (those had decreased when Anita was born but, increased again after the birth of our sons) I was so thankful for my children. My husband never raised a hand to the children or harmed them in any way, and was actually a good father to them, something I was also very thankful for.

Grandmother-Teacher-Friend

Chapter 6

A gray head is a crown of glory; it is found in the path of righteousness.
Proverbs 16:31

Grandma and I became very close after my daughter Anita was born. We talked to each other every day and she taught me many things. There was a lot to learn from her. She had run the boarding house so she was very good at cleaning and knew plenty about cooking, and raising children, after all she had raised three children of her own and two grandchildren. Grandma was an excellent cook, but while I was living in her home she was too busy running the boarding house to teach me to cook, therefore I was not allowed to cook. She was getting up in years and the house on Parkview Place had become to much for her to take care of. The hospitals in the neighborhood

Anchored In His Love

Grandma

were pressing her to sell the house. They needed space to build a parking garage.

We talked many times about her moving in with me. I had a spare bedroom but, Grandma wanted her own separate quarters and she decided to build onto my home so she could have the room she wanted. This situation bothered me. I didn't want the rest of the family to think I had done something to entice her to do this and, I didn't want any problems for her or me. She insisted on building an addition and contracted a contractor to start the project.

She had a lovely addition built with a bedroom and bath as well as a small living room so she could have her privacy. It breaks my heart but, she had anything but privacy or peace after she moved into my home. Her two sons, one of which was my father, would call her daily and spend hours on the phone with her telling her what a big mistake it was for her to have sold her home.

It didn't matter that the neighboring hospitals contacted her constantly wanting her to sell her property so they could expand theirs. My father and uncle also didn't take into consideration that the neighborhood wasn't suitable for an elderly woman living alone, or the fact that maybe she didn't want to live alone and might have enjoyed a little company now and again.

The jealousy started and for six weeks they caused her so much misery she become ill. She was due for an annual check up and went to the hospital to get one...*she never returned home.* Once she was admitted to the hospital my uncle Kenneth would not let any of the family visit her and, he tried to brainwash her into making a new will.

When my Uncle Kenneth called and told me she was gone I was crushed and miserable. In my opinion Grandma died alone at the hospital, of a broken heart. Grandma and I had become close, as I said earlier, and I cherished our time together knowing she was old. I wanted to have as much time as possible with her to glean from her wisdom and enjoy this new level of friendship we had developed since the birth of Anita.

My father and his brother were never close and there had always been tension when they were both in the same room. Jealousy is an awful thing and can destroy families unless it's nipped in the bud. Someone in the family planned the funeral and the services were held at my home church, Gibson Heights Presbyterian Church. The family was divided—some in the back of the church and some in the front. At the time I truly did not know that there was something going on behind the scenes, but there was something brewing and as soon as Grandma was laid to rest some of the family members came against me. They thought I had stolen some of my grandmother's things. Later the truth came out and it was discovered that it wasn't me but it was my Uncle Kenneth. He had forged my father's signature and had stolen some stocks and money that belonged to my father. What a mess the whole thing had become.

My cousin Joanie and her husband, George, were so kind to me during this whole ordeal. They assured me they would always be there for me. It was a great comfort to me during that time to know that I had someone in my family who would stand by me, knowing it wasn't me or my fault.

I was pregnant with Todd when my grandmother died. The sadness of her death was compounded by the fact that she had wanted to see and be a part of this little baby's life.

During the same time frame in which the situation with the stocks and stolen money had occured, that I was not aware of, my Uncle Kenneth called me and we went out to lunch. He told me this would be the last time I would see him and I was in disbelief. I asked him to please not leave and do that to me, but he said they were leaving and not coming back. I didn't know he was the one responsible for the theft and everyone's mistrust of me. My Uncle Kenneth and his wife left town and no one has ever heard from them since.

Our grandmother's death made a relationship with our father all the more important to both Michael and me. We wanted him to be a part of our lives and his grandchildren's lives as well. Michael was a police officer and my dad was proud of him. During the funeral my father befriended Michael, but held me at a distance because of the whole addition to my house ordeal. After the funeral there was still the stolen stocks and money issue, caused by my Uncle Kenneth that didn't come out until later, that also caused my father to steer clear of me and gravitate towards Michael.

While Michael and my dad were bonding together, Michael also stayed away from me. I was crushed and could not comprehend why a person had to choose one family member over the other. It's like saying if I want to love you I can't love the other or vice versa, it made no sense. The period of isolation from my brother and the rejection of my father during this time was a very difficult period in my life.

The Truth About Michael

Chapter 7

"The Lord is good. When trouble comes, He is a strong refuge. And He knows everyone who trusts in Him."
Nahum 1:7

One night when my youngest son was two years old, I received a phone call from my sister-in-law telling me that I needed to go to the hospital because Michael was very ill.

When I got to the hospital I was shocked to discover that my brother was extremely ill and they didn't expected him to survive through the night. I was told he had gone to the emergency room the week before with flu-type symptoms, and after examining him the hospital sent him home. Surprised they would send him home, my brother asked them if he had to be dying before they would admit him into the hospital.

One week later he was back at the hospital and that time they admitted him but, by this time he was in grave condition. My thirty-two year old brother was lying in a hospital intensive care room almost lifeless. I was so upset. Oh, how I prayed that my brother wouldn't die. After calling me to come to the hospital it seems Michael's wife had left. Because of her absence and since I was his sister, the hospital asked me to call our father. It was evident to them that they were losing Michael.

I called our father's home and spoke with his girlfriend. I explained the situation but, before my father would come to the hospital, he called the hospital to verify that what I had told his girlfriend was true, then and only then did he make his way to the hospital.

The family feud, still unresolved at this time, that had started with my grandmother's room addition to my house and fueled even more by the stolen money issue caused by my uncle, is why my father called to verify Michael's condition before coming to the hospital. We had not spoken to each other for some time. He and Michael were on speaking terms but he wanted to make sure what I was telling him was the truth. It had not yet come to light that it was my uncle who had taken the money and my father still thinking it was me, mistrusted me.

While I was waiting for my father to come, two nurses and a doctor came out to talk with me and my husband. They informed us that my brother had died.

The Truth About Michael

My first feelings were of shock and disbelief. When Michael's wife returned to the hospital soon after he had died, the job of telling her about Michael's death fell to me.

I then had to repeat the whole thing over again when my father arrived at the hospital. After hugging my father, I told him that Michael had died and my father fell to his knees. Seeing my father's reaction and his pain was very difficult for me but there was nothing I could do to ease the pain we both felt at this time. Little did I realize that I was in the middle of a nightmare that would only get worse before it got better.

During this time, the hospital staff asked me if any one in my family had a blood disorder. I remembered about two years before when I had been very ill I had been told I might have Leukemia. A bone marrow test was done at that time, and although I did not have Leukemia, I was diagnosed with Leukopenia, which is a condition of the white blood cells. The doctors continued to ask me a lot of questions because they said my brother had died of Leukemia.

> *Little did I realize that I was in the middle of a nightmare that would only get worse before it got better.*

Michael's wife and I went home to my house from the hospital and began planning my brother's funeral.

Anchored In His Love

My brother had been a homicide detective for the police department and they sent an officer each day to help us with any needs that might arise. They offered to assist us in any and everything we might need or ask of them. They helped with the most menial of things down to driving us to the grocery store. At the funeral, the police department had an honor guard standing at each end of the casket.

Every police department in town and surrounding areas was represented at the funeral. There were so many people at his funeral that there was standing room only. The only person I wanted to be with was my father. I knew he would be the only one who could possible feel the same level of pain I was feeling. My father was very distant though, dealing with his own feelings of loss and the already strained relationship because of the family feud. I desperately wanted my father to hold me and tell me he would always be there for me but, that didn't happen. Instead, I felt rejected. This combined with the loss of my brother was like a double mourning.

After the funeral, Michael's wife invited the family to their house for lunch. I was too upset to eat. To make matters worse, I got very upset when I saw Michael's widow and her family acting like it was a party! They were all laughing and joking about Michael being gone and how his widow could now start a new life. She noticed how all the talk and laughter was upsetting me and she got them to settle down. I would later

The Truth About Michael

understand why they all reacted they way they did.

The day after my brother's burial, I received a phone call from the homicide department. They told my husband to brace me for what they were about to say. Apparently, Michael had been murdered. He had been poisoned with arsenic like that found in rat poison, and they had arrested his wife for his murder! Murder! For his murder! They explained they had taken hair samples from Michael at the funeral home, to be tested and the results showed his death had been caused by the poison.

Since Michael's wife was my friend and had even been the maid-of-honor at my wedding, I begged the officers to let me see her. **I absolutely could not believe she would take Michael's life**. They had to have the wrong person.

It just wasn't making sense to me, and I needed answers. Apparently Michael, as sick as he was, had told his colleagues that if anything happened to him to check out his wife. An expert in fingerprinting, his colleagues also consulted him on several other cases while he was hospitalized and Michael helped solve them before he died.

He had recently graduated from school, and was planning to become a prosecuting attorney after passing his bar exam. In his home, he had lots of books and term papers showing how murders were done and solved. One book, in particular, told how to murder someone with arsenic poisoning. The book explained that the symptoms of this type of poisoning are much the same as the symptoms of Leukemia.

It finally came out that Michael's wife had a boyfriend that she intended to marry after Michael's death and she wanted the life insurance money, the house and everything else that came with it. The irony of it all was that she learned how to kill Michael from the textbooks he had gotten from school during his studies.

Michael and his wife had four children, two of them had died in infancy. Michelle was only three and a half months old when she died, and Lisa Marie had been three and a half years old when she died. The bodies of Michael's daughters were exhumed to determine if they had been murdered. Autopsies showed that Michelle died of Sudden Death Syndrome (SDS) and Lisa had a lung problem.

The police department advised me that I should try to get custody of Michael's two other children, a boy and a girl. At this time, Michael's daughter was only eight months old and was in the same hospital where he had died. My husband and I did as the police department suggested and applied for guardianship of my niece and nephew. We were granted temporary custody of both children. My niece wasn't ready to be released from the hospital but we were able to pick up Michael's son the next day.

Within a few days, we were contacted and told that we would have to bring the little boy back to children's services, because Michael's widow had gone berserk

The Truth About Michael

in the hold over cell when she learned we had custody of her son. She was sure we would talk badly about her to the children and she couldn't handle that. So, unfortunately, both my niece and nephew were placed in foster care outside of the city. I was so devastated because I had lost my brother, nephew and niece all at the same time.

My sister-in-law was eventually convicted of first degree murder and sentenced to life in prison for taking Michael's life. At that time, a life term meant seven to eleven years, and in real terms, she only had to serve about nine years of her sentence. While in prison she went to college and got an associate's degree. Also, while she was in prison she got married, not to the boyfriend she killed my brother for but, a different man. They subsequently divorced while she was still in prison.

The social services required the foster parents to bring the children to visit her. I would go visit her during those times as well, because it provided an opportunity for me to see my niece and nephew. She was allowed to have weekend passes and once even came to visit me. When she was released from prison, she remarried for a third time and he died. After the death of that husband she remarried once more and moved to a small town, away from the city where I live.

Getting back to Michael's little girl, when she was released from the hospital, she was sent to stay in the foster home of a Christian couple, who eventually had two daughters of their own. After staying with them for almost her entire life, the social services told the couple that my niece was going to be moved to a different foster home.

Even though they had two daughters of their own they asked to adopt her. My ex-sister-in-law signed the papers on two conditions; one that she would still be her mother and be allowed to have a relationship with her and the other condition was that I would still be her aunt and her brother her brother. This couple agreed to the conditions and were allowed to adopt her. As I said before she had been a part of their family almost her entire life.

My nephew, who looks just like his father, is now a police detective like his father was, and has a daughter of his own.

The Truth About Michael

My Brother Michael

Catastrophic Counsel

Chapter 8

Trust in the Lord with all your heart, And lean not on your own understanding.
Proverbs 3:5

During the whole time of dealing with the death of Michael and losing my niece and nephew, I was still coping with a marriage that despite any efforts on my part to improve as a wife and mother, was not getting better. My husband and I had begun going to a church nearby and we had met a couple that had started ministering to him and counseling with him. I don't know what things he said during those times of counseling but, as I understand it they advised him to take the children and leave. I came home from work one day and he and the children were gone! I had no idea where they were or why he had left. I called my mother-in-law and anyone I thought who could give

me a clue as to where they were but, I got nothing. I was frantic!

I tried going to the school to get my children and they were not there. He had taken them out of school and anyone who might know where they were kept it from me. The people at the church obviously based on what he had told them felt the kids and my husband were better off without me and wouldn't tell me anything. It was if they had vanished.

This went on for months and I was beside myself. I had to work to keep from going crazy and to have a place to live. I didn't have a lot of money but I did have good friends. My employer was so very kind and he did all that he could do to help me.

My husband soon filed for divorce and custody of the children. I had to find an attorney. My friends where I worked helped me get one. The attorney went to work and so did my God. The Lord is so faithful. You see the Bible tells us that God will vindicate us and that He is our salvation. Many people think that only means salvation from sin but, He saves us from the snare of the *enemy who comes to kill, steal and destroy* (John 10:10).

The devil has tried so many times to destroy me through one affliction, trial and test after another and I'm sure he thought he had me this time but God is faithful and if you remember the scripture in the beginning of my book, Jeremiah 25:11 says, *"I know the plans I have for you and they are plans of good and to prosper you..."* God has a plan for me and He will see that I prosper and not perish. He was the Judge that day and He ruled in my favor. After many months of not seeing my children, I finally got them back and was divorced from my husband with custody of my children.

Sixteen years of a marriage that had always been a struggle was now over. I realized that my marriage had been out of the will of God because I had not sought Him on who I was to marry. I reacted out of fear and not faith in the God who had always sustained me. But, now I was ready to build my own life. It wasn't a rebuilding because I had never really had the fortitude to build a life on my own before now.

> *God has a plan for me and He will see that I prosper and not perish. He was the Judge that day and He ruled in my favor.*

During the next few years, while I was raising my children on my own, there were different times when my ex-husband would attempt to take them away from me. Situations arise with children that really have nothing to do with how a parent is raising or training their children, they make choices everyday we would not make for them or condone. My children were no different.

Based on some of the choices my children had made, my ex-husband called the Division of Family Services (DFS) on me and they had to investigate into the type of care I was giving the children and their environment. Each time they would see nothing wrong with how I was taking care of the children.

Sometimes I think he would just do those things as an act of revenge towards me. We would continue to have these struggles throughout the years but I'm happy to say we are really quite good friends today. We worked through our issues and we are not only friends but, he and my new husband are good friends as well.

If I could offer any suggestions to couples who are divorced or going through a divorce keep one very important thing in mind. The children. They didn't ask for their parents to be divorced, most children want their parents to remain married. Love needs to abound toward your children more than ever. Put aside your differences and make the children a priority. They should never feel they have to chose or defend one parent over another.

Don't spend your time trying to hurt your ex-spouse, instead find ways to make your children's lives richer and treat their other parent with respect and honor and the children will learn honor and respect for you.

God's Greatest Gifts

Chapter 9

*Behold children are a heritage of the Lord,
The fruit of the womb is a reward
Psalm 127:3*

      *I*t is hard to believe that children grow up so quickly and become adults, in what seems such a short time, and it is hard for me to believe mine are grown with children of their own.

Raising three children by myself was not an easy job. At times, I worked two jobs and attended college at night. If I bought food, I could not pay my bills and if I paid my bills there was hardly enough to buy food. God had a plan for me and blessed me with a job at a large electrical company in St. Louis, MO.

The CEO at the company was so kind to me and was like a father who always looked out for me. In fact, he encouraged me to finish college, so I enrolled and started taking classes at night. While I was attending night classes at a college, I took math for two and half years, and he actually helped me with math problems that I was stuck on. Every day he would ask me what grade I made on a math test and tell me that he was so proud of me when I told him the grade. I am so thankful to God for allowing me to work for this company and the friendships I made.

I was employed with this company for about sixteen years. While working there they provided me many opportunities to learn and to expand my knowledge. After working there for two years, they taught me how to manage the employee benefits. After becoming proficient at it I became the Benefit Administrator and this is the career I came to enjoy and still function in that industry field today. They even sent me to school so I could get my license in benefits. It was the best experience that I could have and it helped me financially while raising my three children alone.

When they discovered that I was having a tough time making ends meet they told me they needed someone to open the switchboard early in the morning and to stay and close it later in the evening and they asked me if I would do this for them. I eagerly said yes! This extra work helped me stand on my own feet and raise my children.

One year my old car was on it's last leg and I could not get a loan. The company heard about this situation and they sold me one of the leased cars from their fleet. They took the payments a little at a time out of my paycheck so I would have transportation to work. God takes care of every need in your life if you let him. In every circumstance that I went through, I tried to practice a joyful attitude. Many times, I was misunderstood because I was so naive. This was painful but, God was developing me into the person I would become.

One Christmas the company I was working for gave me a free YMCA membership so I could go and take my children. This membership became one of my children's most enjoyable entertainments.

Anita was a huge help to me. She would watch the boys until I returned at night. Time passed and Anita went to college. One of the hardest days of my life was when I drove Anita to college. I had to leave my little girl for the first time and to return home without her was painful. I cried almost all the way home but Todd stepped up to the plate and said, "Mom I'll do the dishes for you now". How precious to hear these words coming out of his little mouth as if to say…I'm here for you mom. We will be okay.

Anita is one of the blessings in my life that only God could have given me. Since I did not know how to be a mother, in some ways, we grew up together. Anita was born with asthma and most of the time she had to play indoors. One day when she was about three years old I let her play out in the back yard for just a moment. I went inside to get something for her and when I returned to the back yard Anita was gone!

The sick feeling that goes through you when your child is missing is unexplainable. I called 911 to report that my child was missing and then immediately called my brother who worked for the homicide division. Because of my brother about twenty-five squad cars were immediately on the scene. There had been several boys kidnapped in our area in the past few weeks which made it all the more frightening.

About an hour later the police brought Anita home, unharmed with a bag of candy and a dollar in her hand. From that time on, I never took my eyes off my little girl again. *"I sought the Lord, and He answered me, And delivered me from all my fears"* Psalm 34:4 and *"The righteous cry and the Lord hears, And delivers them out of all their troubles"* Psalm 34:17 God is so good!

When she was growing up she did not play with dolls a lot but, she loved to read. She would read everything she could concerning the heart. When she was in school she wrote an excellent report on the heart. She helped me unselfishly with the boys. Due to her asthma and the fact that she could not play outside like other children, Anita took piano lessons for twelve years. The lessons and practice hours helped to fill her time.

Since she was ten years old she wanted to be a heart doctor but, in college, she majored in nursing. While away at college, Anita and I became even closer and she encouraged me always. She majored in nursing and the nursing program she enrolled in at the college was a three year program. Many nights she would only sleep for three hours and then get up and study again.

After graduation Anita got a job in the Intensive Care Unit (ICU) of a hospital. I was very proud of my daughter. Many children who come from families with the income we had would not have continued their education. After a few years had past, she accepted a job as Director of Nurses at a local nursing home in Hannibal, Missouri.

Anita married her college sweetheart, Jamie (her soul mate) and they live their lives for the Lord. Jamie lived in New London, Missouri, which is close to the college they both attended. He is a gifted singer and the worship leader at a local church in Hannibal and works as an insurance adjuster during the week. I love Jamie like a son.

They were married about ten years before they were blessed with two beautiful girls, Hannah Grace and Olivia Anne born two and a half years apart. Anita home schools the girls. Olivia is petite, out going, and all girl. She cannot get enough of doll babies. She mothers every child she comes into contact with who will let her.

Hannah on the other hand is tall and a quiet child who is very sensitive. She enjoys making crafts. Hannah also takes piano lessons and is good at it. The

girls are inseparable. They enjoy taking swimming, piano, and dance lessons. Anita is a woman that every one looks up to. She is a role model to follow. Her brothers and she are very close.

Todd lived with me, along with his cat Buffy, a black and white female, a sweet little cat that he had found when he was in grade school. Todd protected me, he felt he was the man of the house being the oldest son and me a single parent for all those years.

Todd was a quiet child. He enjoyed baseball and sports. His favorite football team was the Philadelphia Eagles. He knew all the players to the extent of knowing which high school they attended. Todd and I would play catch almost every day after I came home from work, as he loved baseball, and so did I. He was an excellent swimmer, so when we could, we went to the pool in the summer and what did we do... we played catch together in the pool! Todd also was a Cub Scout and I became a Cub Master and anxiously waited each week to be with the kids. I enjoyed it as much as Todd did I think.

When Todd started high school there appeared to be a change in him. I didn't notice it at first but, the principal started calling me weekly to see if Todd was ill. He was falling a sleep in class and his grades were dropping. The principal asked me if Todd was smoking marijuana. I assured him this was not the case. He asked me if anything was happening around the house. I told him that my house was being Tee-

Peed pretty often and it was annoying but, I couldn't see how that would have anything to do with it.

The principal of the school suggested I take Todd to a specialist to have a check up. I made an appointment for him. The doctor said Todd might be smoking pot and if this was true I needed to get him into a rehabilitation center. He told me I could call him on his exchange if I needed him but, Todd would have to tell me himself about the pot.

I confronted Todd about this issue but, he was not ready to talk about it then. On Sunday afternoon of that same week the singles group at my church had a get together and we ended up at my house. While we were on the front porch, Todd came out and said he needed to talk to with me.

I excused myself and we went inside where we could talk privately. He said, "Mom, you are my mother and you have always said I could come to you about anything. Mom, I need help…I'm on drugs". I stayed calm on the outside but my insides were racing. My goodness, I thought I must have failed him in some way. I asked God to forgive me for not being a better parent. This was a hard situation to be going through alone. I called the doctor right away and the next morning Todd was admitted for rehabilitation for marijuana.

I called Todd's father, who had remarried, to keep him informed. Todd was in rehab for about six weeks or more and was happy and well. The day Todd was

Anchored In His Love

released from rehab, I received a phone call from DFS saying Todd's father had called to report me for not being a good parent.

When Todd heard this he got very quiet and would hardly talk. He said, "Why did he do this to us?". The Division of Family Services dismissed the phone call after talking with me but, the damage was done.

Todd did not want to return to the high school he had been attending when he was on drugs so, I enrolled him in a Christian high school not far from our home. Todd was not well received at this school. The other parents were not happy that I was a single parent and that Todd had just gotten out of rehabilitation for drugs. This did not help the healing process for Todd and for me it was a revelation of how people stereotype a single mother. I had thought that school would be the answer but, after one semester Todd returned to public school.

After graduation Todd moved to Hannibal to live with his sister for the summer and started college in Hannibal that fall. Hannibal is a small town north of St. Louis.

When Richard, someone very special to me that I will discuss in the next chapter, came into my life he was a blessing for Todd and treated him like a son. He made a promise to Todd that if he kept his grades up in college he would take him to the Caribbean and they would sail on his sailboat. Richard had a forty-four foot Highless 400 sailboat, which he named Kokomo.

Todd worked very hard that semester in college and Richard kept his promise to Todd and we all flew to St. Thomas for two weeks to go sailing. Richard taught Todd everything related to the boat and how to sail it. Todd enjoyed every minute of the trip. This was a wonderful experience for Todd, one he will never forget.

During his second year of college, Todd called to tell me that I was going to be a grandmother. Oh my goodness, I was busting at the seams to think that my son who had been there for me no matter what and had never said an unkind word to me, who in my eyes was still just a little boy, was going to be a father.

Months seemed to pass quickly and the day came when Brandon was born. What a special day it was for all of us. There was so much excitement in the family. This beautiful little boy that was brought into the world was just starting his life. I prayed to God when Brandon was born and asked God to let this little bundle of joy learn the ways of God early in his life.

Todd decided to drop out of school at the end of the semester, for only a season, to work and take care of his new family. After a while, he enrolled in a trade school to finish his education. Todd made good grades and graduated with a degree in electrical maintenance.

Todd now has three little boys. He has full custody of two of them. Dawson is small for his age, bright and

 *Anchored In His Love*

tender hearted. While being on staff at a large church in St. Louis, Missouri, I enrolled Dawson in pre-school for two and a half years. He was taught early in his life values that I believe will last him a lifetime. He is a child that anyone could take in their home and enjoy. He is laid back, quiet, and fun.

Brandon, the oldest of the three, is the socialite. He never runs out of things to talk about and is very interested in life. He needs to know how things work and is a good reader.

Michael Todd, is the youngest. He loves his older brothers dearly. He is Dawson's shadow and looks up to Brandon. The three boys enjoy playing wifflelball in Grandma's backyard and Grandma can play with the best of them.

Todd still is a quiet son who enjoys sports more than anyone else I know. He works hard to support his family and would never let anyone hurt me. He sometimes gives a gruff outside appearance but, is a teddy bear on the inside.

Children are special and not everyone can have them. I feel children are a gift from God. The desire of my heart was to have another child and God blessed me with a son, which I named Rodd.

Instilling faith in a child is perhaps the greatest privilege in the world. When Rodd was small I took him to the nursery at my church and to my amazement one day the teacher stopped me when I was about to pick him up after the church service and she said,

"Sandi you have a special child here". I looked at her and said, "he is special to me". She told me that she thought he was so sweet, and that as small as he was, he tried to comfort the smaller children that were crying. She said each week he tried in his own way to be a caregiver. Rodd is a talker and loves to communicate but, is also a sensitive person. When he was growing up God was very important in his life.

When the children's father left me, I didn't have a clue we were going to get a divorce. One day I came home from work and found him gone and he had taken the children. Nearly everything was gone even the sheets on the beds. He left me with ten dollars that he placed on the counter top. The divorce was very hard on the children but especially on Rodd. He tried to do everything he could to reunite us.

I did get my children back but Rodd was restless. He wanted both of us with him. One day I came home from work and Todd was very upset and said Rodd had gone to live with his father. His father had gotten Rodd while I was working without me knowing it. My heart fell out of my chest at that moment. I felt betrayed and I was hurting for a son that was gone. I prayed and asked God to help me because this problem was too big for me to handle. Todd was hurt deeply and felt the pain for weeks, perhaps months, over the situation. He missed his brother terribly. Sometimes you have to let go and let God deal with the issue. I wasn't sleeping and was eating little, so I had to give

 *Anchored In His Love*

the situation to the Lord. When things are falling apart, put your trust in our unshakable God!

One day after Rodd had grown into an adult, he and I were reunited. It was very difficult to re-establish a relationship because his father had turned him against me, and he was raised by a stepmother that wouldn't even let him call me mom. Eventually Rodd got to know me and realized that I loved him and that we both missed out on a lot during our separation. Rodd and I are very close now and he tells me how much he also hurt while he was gone. God is always ready to comfort and sustain us and did this for me during this season in my life. He is also a God of restoration and He brought restoration between Rodd and myself and I thank Him and give Him praise for this.

Rodd has several dogs that he loves and cares for. He takes pride in a clean house and has a knack for knowing how to take nothing and make it into something special. He gives out of his need to others when he knows they need a helping hand. When you have a friend with Rodd, you have a loyal friend who will always be there for you.

In a mother's eye your children are always your babies. Yes, you know they are adults but, a mother's love is so strong that nothing could shake that love. I would lay down my life for any of my children.

During the hardest times in my life I felt God's protection. He sets boundaries in our life to protect us. The Holy Spirit helps you discern between right

 *God's Greatest Gifts*

and wrong, protecting you from evil influences. Life has not always been easy for me but, I ask God to lead me by the hand to His place of safety. God was my Father, He was always there for me around the clock, day in and day out. He never got tired of hearing my voice and was happy when I called on Him. God offers healing and hope when we come to Him. Take comfort in knowing you are in the Savior's thoughts right now. Let God do the fighting for you.

Rewind And Start Again

Chapter 10

Therefore, if anyone is in Christ, he is a new creation; old things have passed away; behold, all things have become new.
2 Corinthians 5:17

In the new life I started for myself I really didn't see marriage again as part of the plan. Nearly ten years went by when a friend of mine from Belleville, Illinois asked me to talk with a man who had just gone through a bad divorce. I wasn't thinking at all about dating or meeting anyone, especially not someone fresh out of a bad divorce, goodness no! I was very hesitant at first but, finally through their persistence I said I wouldn't mind just talking to him over the phone from time to time. This is how I first met Richard, a man who would be part of my life for the next few years.

 *Anchored In His Love*

Within a month of our first phone conversation Richard asked me to go out to dinner with him. I still wasn't ready to meet him but I agreed. When Richard first came to pick me up he wasn't anything like I had expected. The man I saw when I opened my door was short, bald and wore horn-rimmed glasses. During our long phone conversations, I had met a man with a warm, caring heart and in my mind he looked much different. Not to say that a bald man with horned rim glasses cannot be warm and caring, it's just not how I had envisioned him!

We started seeing each other weekly and he took me for long car rides to places I had never been before. We would drive for hours and just talk and talk. As the months went by a friendship blossomed that eventually turned into a love affair.

I knew he would do anything for me and the feeling was mutual. We enjoyed each other's company immensely and had so much fun together. My children loved Richard and enjoyed his friendship as well. I felt so blessed with this special friendship at this time in my life.

Richard had done well for himself and he had invested his money wisely. He lacked or wanted for nothing, and he could and did offer me the moon. He owned a yacht in the Caribbean and we sailed often going to places that many people only dream about.

After one trip to Las Vegas with Richard and his parents I received a phone call from my son, Todd.

Rewind And Start Again

He had a financial need and I had no way to help him. When I hung up the phone I was crying. I got down on my knees and prayed asking God for someone rich to die and bless me with some money so I could help my children. I know that sounds terrible and I wasn't really thinking rationally, my son was in dire need. I could only think that I needed to help him. Asking Richard for money was something I never did.

Within a few hours the phone rang. It was my cousin, Joanie. The first thing Joanie asked was if anyone was with me. I told her that Richard was with me. That's when Joanie told me that my father had died while I was on vacation with Richard and my father's girlfriend had already buried him.

I was so uncontrollably upset with this news that I screamed and threw the phone across the floor. As I explained that my father had died and was buried before I got home, Richard tried to comfort me. He picked up the phone and talked with Joanie who explained that a letter from an attorney had been sent to me requesting me to contact him regarding my father's estate.

I checked my mail and found the letter. The whole situation threw me into a state of shock. I needed to contact the attorney all the while thinking that my father was dead and buried and now I would never have the opportunity to see him again.

A few days later, I was meeting with the attorney to go over my father's will. I quickly discovered that my father, who had been so cold on the outside, had been a teddy bear on the inside and, had loved me dearly but couldn't, or wouldn't show it. My father left me enough money to help Todd, pay off my home and, buy a car which I desperately needed.

Although I was grateful to God for giving this money to me, which had made life easier for me and my children, it wasn't what I really wanted. If I could have had a relationship with my father while he was alive and have my children know him, that would have been the greatest blessing. I did not want this blessing at the expense of losing my father, at the cost of his life, regardless of what I might have prayed. Have you ever had an irrational moment and later wished you could take it back? That's how I felt.

> *I was so uncontrollably upset with this news that I screamed and threw the phone across the floor... my father had died, and was buried before I got*

I obviously was distraught over not being able to attend my father's funeral. It's not like I hadn't known him at all or didn't want to know him. I had at least known my father and while I realized we had unusual circumstances in our family, I always thought we would resolve any issues and at least be able to visit and talk. He and Michael had managed this and I had

Rewind And Start Again

hoped for the same. Now that wasn't going to happen. I just wished I would have had the opportunity to say goodbye at his funeral. How crazy was this that I wasn't even notified!

The attorney shared with me, that in addition to leaving me an inheritance, my father had also left each of the fifteen people who lived in his apartment complex a thousand dollars. He left each of my children a thousand dollars as well. I was touched because my father had never known my children. I thought these gestures were so kind and thoughtful. The Bible says in Proverbs 13:22, *"A good man leaves an inheritance to his children's children"*. I felt proud and honored that this generous man was my father.

A few weeks later, I went to my father's house for the very first time to pick up the personal belongings he had left me. I was in awe of where he lived, the furnishings he had, and the holiday cards he kept, which were priceless to me. It seemed my father had kept every card his friends had ever sent him. By reading these cards I could see who his friends were and discovered to some degree the kind of person he was. Through these cards I saw a person, in my opinion, who cared about people. Memories meant something to him, after all he saved the little things like cards! Remember too, he gave everyone in his building a small inheritance as another sign of how he cared for people in general.

Another thing I noticed about the cards he kept

 *Anchored In His Love*

was that they were all funny ones no matter what the season. This makes me believe that he must have had a good sense of humor.

When my father died he had been living with his girlfriend. She was not around when I walked through his home for the first time. As I went through the place, touching what he had touched and holding different objects that he had held in his hands, I realized that these things were so much more valuable to me than money.

I searched for a picture of my father, and to my surprise the only picture he had was a picture of my brother Michael and myself, which had been taken when I was six and half years old, just after leaving the children's home. I saw a side of my father that day, walking through his house, that brought healing to my soul. I saw a man that had loved his children, his friends and people in general. He made provision for me and my children despite the family divisions that had taken place. He could not have been, in his heart, a man of grudges. He was hurt and angry over the issue with my grandmother and didn't speak with me, yet he left me almost everything he had. Perhaps he had regret or needed forgiveness, I don't know but he could have left everything to his friends, his girlfriend, or some organization as so many people do; but no, he remembered me in his death. I choose to believe he loved me and wanted to care for me.

As I looked through my father's house, and thought

back over the years, I realized I had so much love for him. Even though I hadn't known my father like a child should have, I loved him with a love that was deep inside of me and nothing could remove it. Now that I was grown with three wonderful children, I realized I had just begun to understand why my father couldn't be with me and Michael.

Something I didn't know until I was an adult was that my father had been part of a gang. This kept him from playing a part in the lives of his children. As an adult I can look back and understand that my father kept his distance from us because he wanted to protect us. He wanted to keep us safe from people that may have wanted to cause us harm because of his involvement in the gang. Maybe he didn't want us to follow in his footsteps. It's only speculation because I didn't get to ask that question but, again, it's what I choose to think because I like the reasoning.

It was after the death of my father, that I started feeling that something was missing in my life and I felt God pulling on my heartstrings. Although Richard was a kind, giving and, loving man, he lacked one huge quality that was vitally important for a lasting relationship with me, he wasn't a Christian.

I had invited Richard to go to church with me but he wouldn't go. Instead, one weekend, Richard asked me to run off to Las Vegas and get married. Although we did love each other, I knew something wasn't right in our relationship because I wanted to be married in my

Anchored In His Love

My Father - Milton (Mike) Dean Kurtz

own church with God's blessing. I also knew what the Bible said about believers not being unequally yoked to unbelievers. Deep down, no matter how much I loved Richard, I knew I couldn't marry him.

One day, while I was praying, I asked God about my relationship with Richard. I asked for a clear sign telling me what I was to do about my relationship with him. The next week our relationship changed—Richard and I decided to become just friends again. I had discovered that Richard had another female friend at the lake where he had retired to. I visited him there and he would come up to visit me. Discovering that he had another female companion was the clear sign I needed to know we were not to be together. We remained good friends for many years after that. He was a part of our family functions at holidays and my children's lives until he passed away. It had been a difficult decision for me but, I knew I had to stay in God's will, and I learned a valuable lesson. You might wonder why that was a difficult decision. Even though I had discovered this other woman, I knew Richard loved me. Had I agreed to marry Richard he would have ended their relationship immediately. But, I asked for a sign from God and I believe He gave it to me when I discovered that Richard had a relationship with another woman.

My relationship with Richard had been one out of the will of God. Living a life of sin keeps us from receiving God's best for our lives. He wants so much

Anchored In His Love

more for us but when we choose sin over love we cut ourselves off from Him because He is holy and cannot look upon sin. That's why Jesus on the cross asked God why He had forsaken Him. When the sin of the world came upon Jesus, the Father had to look away. Our Heavenly Father is a forgiving Father and He is Love. When I repented and asked God to show me if I was to be with Richard, He forgave me and let me know that Richard was not the man for me. I stepped back into the favor of God and His blessings and soon I would have the will of God for my life come to me.

There is little we can do in our lives that will make us truly happy outside of His will. I had to depend on God for His infinite wisdom to do that and He did not and never has let me down.

You might say it took me long enough to figure that out but, I'm glad I did. Many people never discover God's love for them and go through life wondering what they will do and why they're here. I may have discovered it slowly over the course of many years but, I fully understand that now. I can say that no matter what life throws at me, life is still good because I know the one true God and if I keep my eyes on Him I'll come out on the other side victorious. I hope you have seen that as we've journeyed through my life, I can. If you can't see it yet, keep reading.

Looking back now, I believe the reason I was in Richard's life was to show him the ways of the Lord. Throughout our years together I continued to go to

Rewind And Start Again

church and asked Richard to go with me. I also shared my faith and why I believed in Jesus with him. A few years ago, quite a few years after we became only friends and I had now gotten married, I got a call from his sister telling me that Richard wanted to see me. He was in the hospital with terminal liver cancer.

I went to visit Richard, taking along some of my family members, including my husband Gary. Gary had developed a good relationship with Richard. I remember it as a very sad evening. Richard had been given only three weeks to live. He still didn't know the Lord, and I asked if we could pray with him to give his heart to the Lord. I don't know if he did give his heart to the Lord but, he did pray with us.

I visited him everyday while he was in the hospital. Right before he died he went into the hospice program that allows you to go home and have a visiting nurse to assist you during the final days before you die and allow you to be at home. He went to his sister's home and his daughter asked me to visit him. I did and that was the last time I saw Richard before his funeral. He asked me if there was anything I wanted him to leave me and I told him he had given me everything I had ever needed or wanted from him.

On one of our visits to the hospital Richard confided to my husband that he loved me. My husband's response was that he had already known that. On my last visit to see him he also told me that he loved me. This had always been a hard thing for Richard to say.

 Anchored In His Love

This would be his last and best gift to me, to let me know that he had and still did, love me.

This had been a bittersweet period in my life. I had loved Richard but couldn't marry him. We remained friends and it allowed me to meet the godly man I am married to today.

The Mission

Chapter 11

How beautiful upon the mountains Are the feet of him who brings good news...
Isaiah 52:7a

After Richard and I stopped dating, I missed traveling because this had been a fun part of my life up to now. In the church bulletin I noticed the church was offering a mission trip to Reynosa, Mexico. Anyone who wanted to go could, and be part of a team that would build bathrooms for the poorest people in Mexico. This interested me because I thought this would be a way I could still travel. Little did I know that this experience was going to not only change my world but also, change my life.

The day came when we left as a group for Reynosa. There were about thirty-five people in the bus and I

 *Anchored In His Love*

didn't know anyone. This was God's plan to get me where He wanted me to be. I had spoken to the pastor, who was in charge of the trip, on the phone a few weeks prior and asked him if I could sit in the back of the bus so I could sleep. He said yes, but when I got on the bus the pastor said, "Sandi, I want you to sit up front by me so I can talk to you". Oh no, this wasn't starting out like I had planned at all. I was just along for the ride and talking to strangers wasn't part of my plan.

God had another plan for me that day. He didn't want me to be shy anymore and He wanted me to like myself. His preordained plan for this trip and the course He had set for me was about to play out. The pastor starting talking about what God wanted for us in our life and that He knew me before I was ever born. You see, I always hung my head and didn't look at people because I was so shy. All I wanted was the guy to be quiet, but no, he kept talking and told me I was important to God and said how glad he was that I chose this trip as my first mission trip. All I could think of was that I was in the wrong place at the wrong time. All I wanted was to get off this bus and go home.

When the pastor would get tired and it was someone else's turn to drive, he sat in the middle of the bus and asked me to sit close to him and his twelve year old daughter. Now I felt more comfortable because I can relate to kids. They are fun and non-threatening. His daughter and I became friends quickly and we stayed

The Mission

together the entire trip.

After several days we arrived in Reynosa, Mexico and to my horror I really knew I was in the wrong place at the wrong time. The bus pulled up to the hotel we were going to stay at for a week. Oh my goodness! This wasn't a nice hotel like I had been in for the many years I had traveled with Richard. This was a hole in the wall and it had bugs, big cockroaches, and bars on the windows. The person at the front desk couldn't even speak English. We were issued one towel for the entire week and lucky to have toilet tissue in the room. Oh God help me, I thought this is going to be the longest week of my life.

Within the time span of only a few hours we had to change clothes and meet the missionaries we would be helping to build bathrooms with, Jane and Elton Harris. Little did I know that there were NO bathrooms! This meant there were none for us to use either. It had become too much for me to handle and I broke down and cried.

Jane took me under her wing and said she knew that I needed a friend and she was there to help me get through the week. My thoughts were only about getting out of there as quickly as I could. I had to go to the bathroom and Jane knew I had experienced all I could take for one day and she found a home where they said I could use their bathroom. I was pleased until she showed me that it was a hole in the floor and some toilet paper. As bad as this seemed, it was better than the smelly outhouse that was presented to me first. This was only the beginning of what was going to come next.

That evening we had to attend church with a dirt floor and the people were the poorest of the poor. I was beside myself by now and sat all by myself on the right side of the church so I could observe the situation. Little did I know, in a few minutes, all the children in this little colony would also sit on the right side. You see the adults sit on the left side and the children sit on the right side. Well, here I am sitting with all these children. The children kept smiling at me and I asked them their names in Spanish. I knew enough of their language to get by and they seemed pleased with that.

The night was over and we returned to the hotel to sleep and then early the next morning we were off to build bathrooms. God only knows they needed one—they didn't have any showers or toilets. When we arrived the next morning, we were told that the women wouldn't be helping with the constitutions, just the men.

The women would just sit and talk with the ladies in the colony. Right away I spotted the kids playing with bottle caps; they didn't have toys. Well, you must know that it broke my heart to see these adorable children with almost nothing. I asked if there was a mall close by and to my disappointment they said they don't have malls, only a little store that you could buy

The Mission

small things. I asked permission for several of the ladies to walk to this store. We were given permission to go but we were told to stay together and to come right back.

Off I went to see what the store had that I could bless these kids with. To my shock this little store had almost nothing. As I was getting ready to leave the store empty handed, I noticed a clothes line and the thought came to me that I could buy this and teach the kids how to play double dutch, a jump rope game I used to play and enjoy.

We returned with rope in hand, and the kids and I played all day. They had never played double dutch before and each one couldn't wait to have their turn. Then I asked if anyone had a ball. Only one boy did and he ran home and I found a stick so we could play baseball. In Mexico only the boys usually play baseball, but they went along with me and we all laughed so hard and had so much fun that I forgot for a moment where I was. That night I left the jump rope and when I returned the next day the rope was gone! They have so little in Mexico, and this rope was taken I'm sure to hang someone's laundry on. Jane Harris saw how disappointed I was and they brought me another rope the next day so we could jump rope.

Before I left Reynosa, Jane said she needed to talk to me about something God had spoken to her. She said God wanted to heal me of being shy and not liking myself, if I would let Him. I just looked at

her and wondered how she knew I was so lonely and hurting. She told me that I didn't like myself and that hurt God. After all, she explained, He made me and told me if I would accept myself the way God made me, I would be changed that day. I hated myself at times and wanted to give my life over to God again. So I did accept that day how He made me. You see, everyone thought I was childish, but God made me CHILDLIKE ….not childish…there is a big difference.

From that day on, my life was changed. I am more outgoing and not as shy anymore. Little did I know that God was going to use the children to change me and through this experience they would be changed and come to know my Lord. As the week passed the children were important to me and I found so much beauty in this land with people who had nothing. They had so little compared to what I had at home.

The day came when we had to leave. This was a sad day for me as I didn't want to leave these people. I had fallen in love with these children and them with me and my heart ached to leave them. I knew this wasn't going to be my last time in Reynosa as I ached to be with these people. Jane said if I wrote to them she would give the letters to the little girls that I had grown so close to. This was the start of a life long friendship that is still on going to this day.

I returned many times to Mexico. I hungered to be with the people that I met there. I feel as if I left part of my heart with these people. Two of the children I loved were Brenda and Marisa. They have children of their own now and when Marisa had her first child, a daughter, she named her after me, which I'm told is an honor in Mexico. Baby Sandi is an adorable little girl. God used a place far away from me to change my life forever. The people in Mexico will forever hold a special place in my heart. Because of this experience, many more children accepted Jesus as their Lord. To God be the glory!

God used what is simple in the eyes of the world [me] to build His kingdom. Ask Jesus what He wants to teach you today. Mark 10:17 says, *"As He was starting out on a trip, a man came running up to Jesus, knelt down, and asked, 'Good Teacher, what should I do to get eternal life'".*

If we open ourselves up to what God wants, instead of what we want, we will be much happier. God's plans are always better than our plans and His ways are perfect.

The Mysterious Letter

Chapter 12

In all your ways acknowledge Him, And He shall direct your paths. Do not be wise in your own eyes; Fear the Lord and depart from evil.
Proverbs 3:6, 7

Every year at Christmas time when I was a young teenager living with my grandmother, I would see her take something from the mailbox and hide it. Each year as I got older I became more and more curious.

One Christmas I went to the mailbox and to my surprise there was a letter for me from a stranger. After opening and reading the letter, I was surprised to discover that the letter was from a lady calling herself "Mother". This was confusing to me because no one had ever talked to me about having a living mother.

My grandmother must have noticed that I was upset because she asked me if anything was wrong. She said that I looked ill. I told her that I had just gotten a letter from a lady who said she was my mother. Grandma asked to see the letter and this was the last time I ever saw it, however, I knew from reading the letter that this person calling herself *"mother"* was living in Long Beach, California.

Apparently my grandmother mentioned all this to my father because he called me and told me that he would give me a one way ticket to see my mother if that's what I wanted. Since Grandma's house was the only home I knew since leaving the orphanage, I was frightened and said, "no" and begged that they not send me away. The subject of my mother was not mentioned again for several years.

I longed to know more about this woman in the letter who called herself mother but, I didn't know how to go about doing it. Each year I would wait at the mailbox to see if another letter would come. When I was seventeen years old another letter did arrive and I took this letter and hid it. I didn't say anything to a single soul because I didn't want anyone to take this letter away from me.

I anxiously wrote to my mother at the address she had given me but, instructed her not to write me back at my grandmother's address. Instead, I gave my mother a girlfriend's home address.

In the letter I received, my mother wanted me to come to California to meet her and stay for a visit. The thought of doing this frightened me as I didn't

The Mysterious Letter

know her, and didn't want to lose the family I had. I didn't go at this time but I waited until I was about nineteen years old and then decided to take a bus to Long Beach, California to meet my mother. It was a long ride on a bus and I had never been away from home.

> *My father told me he would give me a one way ticket to see my mother...I was frightened and said, "no"....I begged not to be sent away...but I waited...*

When I arrived at the bus stop in Long Beach, California, no one was there to pick me up. I had to wait a while before my mother finally came. I discovered that my mother was married to an artist named Sam. He was older than she was, with white hair and a white beard. My first impression of her was that she looked young enough to be my own sister. She was slender and beautiful with soft, long blond hair and greenish-blue eyes just like Michael's.

I was excited and frightened at the same time, and our first meeting was not a good one. Loretta Ann, which is what she requested I call her, accused my father of stealing both Michael and I and then hiding us from her. The experience was an eye opener for me—she was miserable. I believe I know why. She had items of the occult in her home. She talked about a third eye and had it framed on her wall. Later in life I would go to California again and this time I would gain even more insight into my mother and the life she lived.

    I realized how very different my life would have been if my mother had raised me. I thank Jesus for taking me out of that situation! The road she traveled was a road of loneliness, hardship, sickness and despair. My mother may have been beautiful on the outside but inside she was hard as nails. The first night I stayed with her and Sam but, the next morning they found a motel close to their home where I stayed for the next few days, until I gladly returned home.

    Several years went by before I made another attempt to know my mother.

The Mysterious Letter

My Mother Loretta Ann

My Other Mother

Chapter 13

My son, hear the instruction of your father,
And do not forsake the law of your mother;
For they will be a graceful ornament on
your head, And chains around your neck.
Proverbs 1:8, 9

Without a shadow of doubt it was my Father God who had brought me through all the difficult times in my life, and without Him I don't know how I would have come through them all.

During these times in my life, my relationship with Thelma, who had befriended me so many years ago at the Presbyterian church near my grandparents home, played a big part in my life as well.

As the years had passed and even when I got married, Thelma and I stayed in touch. During the last eighteen years of Thelma's life, we were inseparable. There wasn't a day that passed that we didn't talk.

 *Anchored In His Love*

I loved Thelma, and she was not only my closest friend but, Thelma had told her family that I was the daughter she had always wanted. Thelma had never married and during the latter years of her life, I believe Thelma needed me as much as I needed her. She taught me that the most important things in life were to know God, to live for Him, to be a blessing to others; to shine His light in everything that I did.

Thelma had confided to me that she had a desire to be in a wedding. So, I told her if and when I ever got married, she could be the mother of the bride. That thrilled her so much. Thelma had always encouraged me to find a Godly husband. I truly believe that Thelma knew her time on earth was ending soon and she didn't want me to be alone.

Because of Thelma's influence in my life and my decision to live my whole life for Him, I believe that God honored that decision, and in time, brought a man who had a heart after Him into my life. His name is Gary. It took almost six years of dating before I said yes to a second marriage. Since I had failed in one marriage and had invested so much time in my relationship with Richard, I was afraid of failing again. I wanted to be sure I was marrying for the right reasons and in God's will.

I also waited to marry because I didn't want to introduce another man into my children's lives. After the years spent with Richard that didn't end in marriage, I felt I should wait until they were grown before marrying again. Besides, while my children

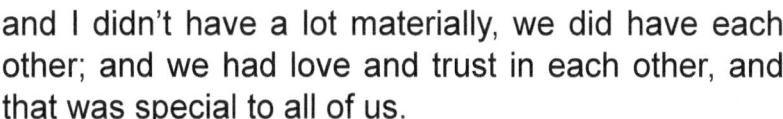
My Other Mother

and I didn't have a lot materially, we did have each other; and we had love and trust in each other, and that was special to all of us.

We had developed family traditions, things we did that were unique to us, that they've carried over into their lives with their spouses and children. Family and tradition built on the Bible and the teachings of Jesus formed who we were as a family unit. Not to say that Gary wouldn't have gladly moved into that unit and melded very nicely, I just wasn't ready to incorporate anyone else into it.

As promised, Thelma was the mother of the bride in my wedding to Gary. She was thrilled and honored and well pleased with my choice to marry Gary. She had wanted me to marry a man with a heart after God and she believed Gary was just that man. I was thrilled she got to be a part of it because one winter night not long after I married Gary, God called Thelma home. That night I had tried calling Thelma several times and got concerned when I couldn't reach her. I had just talked to her a few hours before. I called Thelma's cousin, Dorothy, telling her that I felt something was terribly wrong. Dorothy said that she had just been with Thelma. Since Dorothy didn't have a car, she called her son, who took her to Thelma's house. Dorothy called me back to tell me they had found Thelma lying dead at her back door. Hearing this news, I was overwhelmed with grief and my heart was broken.

 *Anchored In His Love*

The only sweet and precious thought I have of her death is her joy at being with Jesus and knowing I will see her again one day. This is a promise to those who know Jesus as their Lord and Savior. Many have the misconception that as long as we haven't done some heinous crime in our life that all people go to heaven. The sad truth is that good people go to hell everyday because they have not made Jesus the Lord of their life. The Bible tells us in John 3:3 "Unless a man be born again he shall not see the Kingdom of God." There is only one way to heaven and that is through Jesus Christ. If this were not so and we could get to heaven by simply doing good deeds, then Jesus laid down His deity and became a man to die a cruel and horrible death for nothing. Yes, He rose again and sits at the right hand of God the Father but His sacrifice was for nothing if we can attain heaven on our own.

Gary has accepted and loved me with all the things I brought to the table. My three children, my grandchildren, my ex-husband and former lover turned friend, Richard. Gary has embraced my family and made my friends his friends. This is a tribute to the love of God in him and his heart to love me and all that I am. I don't know of many men who would befriend ex-boyfriends and husbands like Gary has. Everyone's life has drama but now I have Gary to support me during those times. I like to think I support him as well and that we make a good team. God knew what He was doing when He gave me Gary. I am grateful for my husband and friend.

My Other Mother

Mary and I on our wedding day,
August 29, 1998

Oh To Know My Mother

Chapter 14

Though I have all faith, so that I could move mountains, but have not love, I am nothing.
1 Corinthians 13:2b

After I grew up and first got married, I tried to reach out to my mother. I would send her a small gift during the holidays. We would exchange letters off and on for years but nothing too intimate like a mother and daughter might share. I had visited her when I was a teenager and now after corresponding all these years I wanted to visit her again. I was divorced and dating Richard during this time. He was going to be in California visiting a friend and he agreed to take me to see my mother. So I wrote and asked if we could come. To my surprise she wrote back with a strong resounding, "NO!"

I didn't understand why she reacted the way she did and why she didn't want to get to know me on a more personal level. I was very hurt by my mother's actions and I stopped writing for a season. She must have associated the cessation of letters to her strong response, because during this time I received a letter from her chastising me for asking to come to see her when she wasn't ready for a visit. In that letter, she told me to never write to her again. She reacted the same way I had to the hurt. She withdrew. Her reaction to my request to visit would never have given me any reason to believe she would be hurt by me not writing but, apparently she was and she withdrew just as I had. I would attempt to bridge the gap now made even wider by giving her love without cause.

From that day on I would drop my mother a postcard each week just to let her know I was thinking about her. I know you're probably wondering why I did that when she said don't write anymore but, love doesn't give up and I loved her, she was my mother. She had not ever done anything to cause me to love her except be my mother. I had apparently sent a wrong message when I quit writing and I wanted her to know I loved her. Love has healing power. She didn't respond to my letters or cards but I would not give up.

One day the urge was so strong to reconnect with my mother that I did a missing person search on her, and found her phone number. I called the number, and to my surprise she answered the phone. When I identified

Oh To Know My Mother

myself, she told me she didn't want to speak to me; she then said goodbye and hung up without saying another word. I tried to call back but she wouldn't answer the phone, so it was no use. Little did I know that this would be the last time I would hear my mother's voice.

One day I had a feeling of desperation to find out if my mother was alright. I couldn't get past that feeling and it pushed me to continue to try and contact her. Once again I did a people search, this time to get a list of any neighbors in her area with a phone number. After much prayer, I called a lady who I thought might live close to my mother. A soft spoken lady answered the phone and I explained that I was looking for my mother who I believed lived near her.

Although the woman was getting ready to leave on a camping trip, she did acknowledge that she knew my mother, and had seen her just the week before using a walker to bring groceries home because she didn't have a car. She also told me that my mother kept to herself most of the time, and had a cat named Lucky. She offered to speak with me again if I would call back after the weekend.

Just a few months later I received an official letter from Los Angeles County asking me to contact them about my mother. The letter explained that my mother had died seven weeks before and they were looking for any relative to claim the body.

I called the phone number on the letter and explained that I had only met my mother twice in my life and both times it had been a bad experience. Nevertheless, I was told to fax my birth certificate and make plans to travel to Long Beach to claim the body of my mother. I was told I would have to make funeral arrangements for my mother and find a burial site.

A few days after the conversation with the lady from Los Angeles County, I received a phone call from a neighbor of my mother's, named Kathy, who lived across the street from her and had known my mother well. That phone call was the beginning of a friendship that will last the rest of my life. Kathy still calls me and I call her even as this book is being written and published. Kathy told me that she had asked the lady from the county to give my phone number to her so she could call me. She offered to help me with everything. She helped me find a funeral home and an attorney. She would look up numbers and names and give them to me so I could decide which funeral home to use for my mother's service.

I was so grateful for this help because this was a difficult time for me, even without the news of my mother's death. I had just lost my job due to budget cuts, and Gary and I didn't really have the finances to fly to California. We live in the Midwest and I had no idea how to go about all the necessary arrangements that were needed for my mother's funeral that would take place all the way on the other side of the country.

In addition to Kathy's help, I was able to find out more information about my mother. I felt that she was the kindest lady I would ever meet, and it was because of her kindness that I booked a flight to California to pursue the next chapter in my life.

Once in California, I met with a representative from the county. Among other things, I discovered that the officials had been able to track me down through the post cards I had been sending my mother each week. I had always put my return address on them, just in case my mother decided to write, and I had signed each one with, "I love you, your daughter, Sandi."

The neighbors were shocked and happy when they first met me. They had all thought Loretta Ann had no relatives. I learned from them that my mother told everyone that she had a son who had been kidnapped when he was younger but, my mother had never said a word about having a daughter.

Since my mother had no will, I needed to hire an attorney to help me fill out the necessary paperwork to be the administer of my mother's estate. I also discovered that my mother had two young male friends at the time of her death. One of them thought he should have my mother's home and belongings and had tried unsuccessfully to get my mother to sign a will, leaving everything to him. Another priority was to get the locks changed on my mother's house because several people had keys to the house and had been taking things out of the house before I arrived.

Using the attorney, suggested by the friendly neighbor, Kathy, I was able to get the necessary

 *Anchored In His Love*

paperwork started. A worker from Los Angeles County found a locksmith to quickly change the locks at my mother's home, because people were still coming and going into my mother's house, taking anything and everything they could carry.

While my husband Gary and I waited for about an hour outside of my mother's home for the locksmith to come, I remember sitting there looking at my mother's home, and being humbled and filled with so much compassion for my mother.

When the locksmith finally came, we went in the back door to make sure none of the neighbors could see what we were doing. While the locksmith was changing the locks on the house, I took my first look around my mother's home and was in awe of my mother's meek life style. I was amazed to discover that the people who had been taking things out of the house had taken so many of her personal possessions. Many of the drawers were completely empty.

After the locksmith left, I just stood in silence for a few minutes then began walking from room to room taking everything in but not touching anything. Just to be in the home where my mother lived was a little overwhelming for me. While I had been to California once when I was nineteen, I still had tried and hoped to visit her again after corresponding over the years with her but, it didn't happen.

The attorney had advised me to take any mail and to look for bills before I left the house. Since Gary

Oh To Know My Mother

and I were staying at a hotel, we gathered up all the mail that was in my mother's house and took it to the hotel to look over. I discovered that my mother was an immaculate person in every way.

Every drawer in her house, that wasn't emptied before I arrived, was immaculate and all her life was laid out on a card table in the living room. Nothing was hard to find. It was as if my mother was trying to say, "Sandi...I made it easy for you." Every deed to her home, every bill... everything was right on this card table in the living room. Unbelievable!

My mother lived a simple life with everything in an orderly manner with little more than nothing to live on. She made daily logs in pocket calendars, which I now have, about trips to visit churches and about groups from local churches and organizations who visited her to pray for her. She logged the simplest of details she performed in a day like washing her hair. She would write about riding the bus or taking her medicines. She logged how much she weighed each week .

In these calendar log books she also wrote about a ghost or ghosts that she referred to as "spooks" that must have visited her regularly, and while not comfortable with them according to some of the logs, she didn't seem to be frightened of them either.

These little calendar/daily logs are treasures that have given me a little insight into my mother's life. I've read through them and laughed and cried over the different notes I've found in them.

Anchored In His Love

			DECEMBER 1994			
1994			Every day in every way, I'm getting better and better.			1994
SUNDAY	MONDAY	TUESDAY	WEDNESDAY	THURSDAY	FRIDAY	SATURDAY
				1	2	3
4 /34 lbs.	5 1:30 p.m. Dr. Garrison Visual Field 7:30 p.m. #3 Earth quake	6	7	8 Rode Bus Went Downtown + Checked out Williamsburg Bakery + Restaurant	9	10

   I've included some small snippets of the calendars because they are now a part of who I am. They have given me a part of my mother that I never knew.

   One of the calendar pictures I've included shows that three spooks sang happy birthday to her on her birthday, December 8th. The reference to this is in the box with a smiley face. This is what led me to believe that she wasn't necessarily afraid of them.

   Next to that daily log, the one in a long outlined rectangular box with a half circle and another little box that juts off of it, is one that makes reference to a birthday card I sent her that arrived *on* her birthday, according to her, for the first time *on time* but that I had used that occasion to inform her of Norma Mitchell's death, an old friend of hers that I had met when Norma was trying to reconnect with my mother because they had lost touch.

   Another calendar picture I've included is where

Oh To Know My Mother

her friend Bryan, someone whom throughout all the calendar logs in this calendar, she is giving or loaning money to, makes reference to the "spooks" telling her to give him her garage. She notes that it's a lie and she hung up on him but first said goodbye and that she'd speak to Cassandra another time.

1995			APRIL			1995
		It is better to be a has-been than one who never was.				
SUNDAY	MONDAY	TUESDAY	WEDNESDAY	THURSDAY	FRIDAY	SATURDAY
						1
2 Daylight Saving Time begins	3	4	5	6	7	8
9	10	11	12	13	14 Good Friday	15 Passover
Palm Sunday						

This little snippet gave me the impression that her friends knew that she was hearing or seeing things she shouldn't and they tried to take advantage of her or perhaps they were all in some kind of cult together. The note on that particular day not only said that the spooks told him to tell her that but that their brotherhood depended on it.

I've also included a calendar picture showing that I called on September 7, 1995 and the little paper

 Anchored In His Love

snippet below it is the note she wrote documenting the call I made that day.

1995			SEPTEMBER			1995
A wise man will make more opportunities than he finds. Francis Bacon						
SUNDAY	MONDAY	TUESDAY	WEDNESDAY	THURSDAY	FRIDAY	SATURDAY
					1	2
3 Deborah Raped Ms. Ralph ho god child	4 Labor Day	5	6 136 lbs. Urica Brought Kittens to Show. Calico was a Cat	7 Sondra Phoned Deborah phoned Washed Hair	8 I Phoned Katy I called Susie	9

Thurs. Sept. 7, 1995. (10 A.M.)

Phone Call — "Loretta Ann. This is Sandi".
Response: Jesus Christ! Excuse me —
I don't want to talk to you!
Caller — "Alright" (Sad Small Voice)

As I was walking from the living room into the next room I saw a large easel and lots of paints, brushes and books. This must have been the room she painted in and everything was still in it's place. Much to my shock and unbelief was a small framed picture of me that I had sent her at one time. This woman, that had

Oh To Know My Mother

been so cruel and heartless to me, had put the picture of me in a place she could see it each day as she sat and painted.

No words can tell you how this little picture touched my heart and life forever. To discover that this woman who had caused me nothing but pain, deep down, in her own way, had loved me. This was such a comfort to me. God filled me with so much understanding and compassion for this little 5' 4 inch petite lady who must have been very lonely.

My mother lived with only a seven inch black & white television. I'm not talking about in the 1960's or 1970's, I'm talking about when she died in 2003. I know this only because one of my mother's gentlemen friends came by while we were there and returned the television. She had one radio, a twin bed, a dresser in the bedroom, a night stand and a lamp. Her closet was so orderly with everything color-coded. Her clothing must have been thirty years old but they were clean. She had little smocks and Indian moccasins that she wore. Every item was clean.... it touched my heart.

My mother's home and furnishings were quite modest by Los Angeles standards. I was surprised to see what a very small home cost in Los Angeles in comparison to where I live. I can't imagine how my mother was able to live in such a place where the cost of living is so high. This must have played into her meager belongings and the renters she took in. Her calendar logs made mention of men moving in, paying

rent, moving out and her refunding money. Some of the logs speak of these men making threats to her such as beating her up. If these were true, I think they must have been she kept good logs pertaining to my phone calls and conversations. I would lean toward believing she dealt with such things.

My mother was a professional artist and sold some of her paintings to the Long Beach Art Museum and they still have them on display to this day. I've included one of the pieces of artwork I found in her home drawn by her. It's a picture of a little girl. Is this a picture of me how she may have imagined I looked as I was growing up, maybe some other little girl? Perhaps it's a self portrait, the sad little girl she really felt inside. I'll never know. I do know this though, her artwork showed

My mother's home in Los Angeles

Oh To Know My Mother

The drawing of the little girl found in my mother's studio

 *Anchored In His Love*

a depth of emotion I never personally experienced from her and I wish I had known the person capable of so much beauty and emotion depicted in her art.

Never Ending Surprisess

Chapter 15

Hatred stirs up strife, But love covers all sins.
Proverbs 10:12

The lady from Los Angeles County threw another surprise my way. She said when she was going through my mother's phone book she had discovered that my mother had two half sisters that lived in Georgia and Alabama.

After she made contact with them it was discovered they had never met my mother but did correspond through letters with her from time to time. It seems that my mother's father divorced her mother and married a lady who was the same age as my mother. This situation hurt my mother and resulted in her being estranged from her father for years.

Anchored In His Love

The two half sisters, Carol and Linda, shared with the lady from the county that they knew of two daughters that were born to Loretta Ann but, knew nothing about my existence and were shocked to hear there was another child born to Loretta Ann that they knew nothing about.

The first names of the two other daughters were Jean and Pamela but, they didn't know their last names. They did, however, know the last name of my mother's second husband, the father of Jean and Pam.

The lady from the County said there was a Christmas card from a Pam Galloway and this perhaps could be one of my sisters. That evening in my hotel room, I called every Galloway in the phone book looking for Pam Galloway. I left messages, hoping to make a connection that would help me discover my sister.

This latest discovery of other siblings now brought up another interesting situation. According to California law when there is more than one sibling in the family of a deceased relative the majority must be in agreement to cremate rather than have a burial. Not knowing at this time how to locate Jean and Pamela, I had to proceed with burial plans.

While making the funeral arrangements it was discovered that my mother's last husband had been in the Coast Guard. This meant that my mother could be buried at Riverside Veterans Cemetery. This was good news and a wonderful blessing from God. My funds, already low from losing my job, were rapidly dwindling.

The expenses for the funeral and memorial service had to be paid for up front, and my husband Gary and I didn't have the money for this expense. We contacted Gary's parents and asked for a loan. They agreed to loan us the money which was to be paid back when the estate was closed. They wired the money and we received it the next day. I was thankful because this meant my mother would have a memorial service and burial.

The funeral director asked me to bring some clothing for my mother to be buried in. The next morning Gary and I went back to my mother's little house to look for something she could be buried in. With tears in my eyes, I searched for just the right outfit. In the back of my mind I wanted something very special for this woman who had suffered so much in her life but, there wasn't much to choose from in her closet. The only clothing in her closet were little thin dusters or smocks that she must have wore daily. The one I chose was rather plain but sweet for the occasion.

My brother's daughter, my niece, had never met her grandmother, although she had tried to contact her several times. When my niece heard about her grandmother's death, she decided that she and her brother needed to come to California to be a part of settling the estate.

I was surprised but, nonetheless thrilled, they were coming. I loved my niece like a daughter and this,

Anchored In His Love

I thought would be comforting to have her with me through the process of settling the estate. After all she was my brother's daughter and as his heirs they had a right to be at the estate hearing. Unfortunately, the situation with my niece turned ugly, and she was anything but a comfort. For some unknown reason she was so afraid of being cheated out of what she felt she had coming or deserved, that she contacted an attorney to represent her interests if necessary. Throughout the whole settling of the estate, she would prove to be more of a distraction and source of strife and contention than a help or comfort. It still grieves me that we cannot recapture the relationship that I felt we once had. I did my best to remain loving and kind.

The funeral director arranged for a memorial service for my mother to be held on a Sunday afternoon at a historical little chapel in Long Beach. It was the most beautiful place that I could have imagined for my mother's service. I was delighted to see that quite a few people, mostly my mother's neighbors, took the time to show respect for her.

A neighbor, named Phyllis, who lived across the street from my mother's home, generously offered to hold a reception for the family and friends after the memorial service. It seems Phyllis had befriended my mother, and now became my friend for life.

This reception was above and beyond anything I could have imagined that a virtual stranger could have

Never Ending Surprises

held for me and my family. We were welcomed into the neighbor's home to meet my mother's other neighbors with open arms. This gave me an opportunity to discover what my mother must have really been like when she was around people she felt comfortable with. I could see the kind of people she enjoyed being with and were her friends.

While I was visiting with the neighbors, I got a phone call on my husband's cell phone. Little did I know that my prayers were about to be answered. To my surprise and delight the call was from a lady who identified herself as Pam Galloway, my sister.

My emotions were running wild inside of me. I was both happy and afraid, I was afraid of being rejected. Suddenly the call was disconnected. I was heart broken because I realized I hadn't gotten Pam's phone number. Thankfully, Pam called back saying she was going to pack a few items and would meet me in the morning. She also told me that she would contact her sister, Jean.

I invited Pam to our mother's burial, which was scheduled for the next morning. Pam informed me that she would not be able to be at the burial because she lived so far away but, plans were made to meet at my hotel later in the day. I had so many emotions going through my mind at that moment. Even though I was happy, I was scared to actually meet my half-sister for fear of being rejected. Rejection has always been a battle for me and the Lord is continually working in me to show me that the root of that rejection is because of the abandonment of my parents and the lack of tender nurturing even from my grandparents; but, that in Him I am loved and accepted. This is a work in progress but I am much further now than I was then.

    The next morning, when Gary and I arrived at the cemetery, we were overwhelmed by it's beauty. Bells were ringing and there were flowers everywhere. We arrived at the burial site only to discover that there would be an hour delay because the grave diggers were not expecting relatives to attend the burial. They went out of their way to accommodate us.

    While we were waiting, I noticed a man with a dog sobbing uncontrollably over a grave. I went over and spoke with him and he told me his wife had died suddenly. I told him I was there to bury my mother and because I didn't live in the area, I would not be able to visit my mother's grave very often. This gentleman told me that he had once lived in St. Louis, and if I wanted, he would visit my mother's grave for me once in a while. This was another gift from God to help comfort me.

    After an hour of waiting Gary, and I were motioned to come to the grave site. The two grave diggers, stood by the grave with Gary and I. We all held hands as I offered up a prayer, and all four of us started crying. These two strangers, that God had preordained for just a time as this, showed us so much compassion. They could have been any two other people and not shown any compassion or simply stepped off to the side but, instead they joined us in our mourning and prayed with us. I choose to believe God touched them that day with my prayer and perhaps some day in heaven I'll know for sure.

There are no words big enough to express the grief and loneliness that I was feeling at this point. I felt very close to my mother at that moment, even though I knew I'd never see or speak to her again. I am very thankful for all the attempts I made to know her and grateful for the opportunity to be at her funeral and say goodbye, unlike my father's death and funeral where I found out too late to attend.

A very unsettling thing did occur during the time at the grave site after we prayed, the lid of the coffin came loose while they were lowering it into the ground. It was rather an odd situation that they would lower her into the ground while we were still there but, they did. The lid on the coffin came open and without thinking, I screamed with horror and one of the grave diggers jumped into the hole and pushed the coffin lid back on.

> *The lid on the coffin came open and....I screamed with horror.*

My emotions were a jumbled mess inside as Gary and I headed back to the hotel after burying my mother. I was going to meet my youngest sister for the first time. When I was a little girl I had prayed for a sister for years to help ease my loneliness. Unknown to me I had a sister, sisters actually, and didn't know it. Yes, they were half-sisters but had we been allowed to interact I'm confident we would have been close.

So much had happened over the course of days leading up to my mother's funeral and burial that I really hadn't had time to process anything. Once the burial had been completed, I felt empty, yet honored that God chose me to carry out this final act of kindness for my mother. My name means "helper of mankind" and I had come to realize long ago that God had given me a soft heart to help others.

Pam and her husband had arrived at the hotel before Gary and I, and when the elevator door opened there were two strangers standing there. Pam's husband looked at me, and said to Pam, she looks like you. Then he turned to me and asked, "Are you Sandi?"

Of course I answered, "yes" and introductions were quickly made amid many hugs. Although I didn't know what my sister thought about me, or if she would reject or like me, I smiled and invited them to my hotel room to visit privately instead of going to the lobby or a restaurant or some other public place.

Pam and I talked endlessly about one thing then another. I relaxed as I got to know my sister and her husband. I showed Pam the papers that I had brought from our mother's home to look through and shared with her everything that had happened up to that moment. Pam made arrangements with Jean, our other sister, to meet at our mother's home that afternoon to talk and get acquainted. I also made sure to contact my niece and nephew to let them know what time we would be meeting.

Pam and I bonded quickly and started a friendship that has grown stronger, even to this day. While we are two different people from completely different backgrounds, we have bonded by love toward each other. I had discovered that one of my mother's male friends and the nurses in the hospital had put pressure on my mother to make a will, knowing her time on earth was short. I felt that my mother had not made a will on purpose as a way to bring her three daughters together.

Later that afternoon, I was once again at my mother's house but, this time I wasn't alone. Pam and her husband, along with my niece and nephew, were with me waiting to meet my other sister, Jean.

I was standing in my mother's art room when Jean finally arrived. I watched as Jean walked through the front door, immediately noticing that Jean strongly resembled my brother, Michael. Jean was tall with blond hair just like my brother and mother. By this time my heart was beating fast and I started to walk toward Jean but, was stopped in my tracks when my niece jumped up and got to Jean first.

I don't know why but I was devastated when I realized that the sister I had so longed for thought my niece was her sister. She probably assumed I was

younger than she was, not realizing that in actuality I was the oldest living sibling. After they embraced Pam stepped in and explained to Jean that she needed to meet "Sandi" who was standing in the art room. I was deeply saddened by the fact that I didn't have the time to really be alone with Jean and bond with her like I had with Pam. Instead we were forced to begin our relationship with the difficult task of deciding what to do with all our mother's possessions. I had to remind myself that this wasn't a real family reunion. It was three complete strangers with a common bond, meeting for the first time in a difficult situation.

I quickly discovered that there were feelings of distrust towards me because I was the first one that had gone into our mother's house and so many of her possessions were missing. Drawers had been completely cleaned out before I even arrived at our mother's home. My niece and nephew were outraged at this situation and did a canvas of the neighbors and friends who knew my mother to find out what they had seen or what they knew.

My niece struck out at me as if I was her worst enemy and told my newly discovered sisters that she really didn't know me very well. Since my brother's death, this niece had been like a daughter to me, so I felt an indescribable pain at hearing these unexpected and betraying words. It felt like someone was putting a knife into my heart. The hurt of burying my mother and all chances for getting to know her and have a

Never Ending Surprises

relationship with her gone, and in the same day, cleaning out her house was almost the breaking point for me. It was compounded when I watched my niece fluttering around the house saying how much fun she was having going through all my mother's things. Although my niece and nephew were entitled to their father's share of my mother's estate, to me, everything seemed to be centered on what they would get. This is something foreign to me. I wanted things that would bring me closer to my mother but not material things for gain.

Later I found out that my niece was forming a relationship with Jean behind my back. Jean shared with me that she found it hard to trust people and I believed this stemmed from the hurts she experienced during her childhood. Jean is a wonderful but, sensitive sister, who has to work way too much just to make ends meet. When my niece heard this she took full advantage of Jean. She convinced Jean to agree to be co-administrator of the estate because she said that I couldn't be trusted.

My niece informed me that if I didn't agree to Jean being co-administrator she would have the attorney block the proceedings. She also demanded that we couldn't take any fee out of the estate for being the administrators. My niece's negative feelings towards me put a wedge between Jean and I. The hurt that I experienced because of this situation was stressful. This was so painful because all I wanted was to be fair to everyone and get the estate settled in the shortest possible time. Anyone who knows me would have told Jean or anyone else that it is not my personality to be selfish or stingy, quite the opposite, I take great joy in blessing others and seeing others happy and blessed.

It was expensive flying back and forth to take care of this estate not to mention the friction between my niece and myself was almost unbearable. As I mentioned before, my relationship with my niece has not been restored and this is a loss I feel very deeply. I had gone out of my way to make sure a relationship was maintained between my niece and myself, even to the point of accepting her mother, despite the fact that her mother had murdered my brother. I did this to ensure that her mother would allow me to see both my niece and nephew.

I can only hope that with time, God will reveal to her my heart, and in spite of the circumstances we can be reunited and our relationship restored. Our family has suffered enough rejection and separation.

There is a happy ending to this story. Through all these trials and tests prayers were answered and the most precious to me is the prayer for a baby sister. I was doubly blessed because I discovered not one baby sister but two. We continue to communicate with each other and are developing a relationship. Pam and I are the closet because as Jean had conveyed when we met, she is slow to trust and this relationship

 *Never Ending Surprises*

has to be more slowly developed. Both my sisters allowed me to take pictures of them and I cherish them. I will not share these photos here because I honor their privacy and the intrusion this would bring into their lives. I know with time, we will come to know and love each other as sisters should. The only regret I have is that they never had the opportunity to meet Michael.

I've written an epilogue to encourage anyone reading my book. I hope you read it and find strength in it. God will do for you what He has done for me. I am an overcomer, victorious, blessed and happy.

Epilogue

Life is a theater. Invite your audience carefully. Not everyone is healthy enough to have a front row seat in your your life. There are some people that need to be loved from a distance. It's amazing what you can accomplish when you let go, or at least minimize your time with draining, negative, incompatible, not going anywhere relationships or friendships. When you leave certain people do you feel better or worse? Which ones always have drama surrounding them, or don't really understand you where you are right now, or appreciate you? The more you seek quality, respect, growth, peace, love and truth around you, the easier it will become for you to decide who gets to sit in the front row of your life and who should be moved to the balcony.

 *Anchored In His Love*

Hold happiness, love, and joy first and this will provide you with a satisfied life. I've learned from my life to treasure a friend. *"If out of all mankind one finds a single friend, he has found something more precious than any treasure, since there is nothing in the world so valuable that it can be compared to a real friend."*

Although we may not be able to prevent the worst from happening, we are responsible for our attitude toward the inevitable misfortunes that darken life. Bad things do happen; how we respond to them defines our character and the quality of our lives. We can choose to sit in perpetual sadness, immobilized by the gravity of loss, or we can choose to rise from the pain and treasure the most precious gift we have – life itself.

God makes Himself known to those who seek His presence. He shares Himself with all who are hungry for Him. Everybody has problems. The devil makes sure that all of us have a stone or two in our lives. Jesus told us that we are to bear the marks of a Christian! The mark of a Christian is not sickness, disease, lack and misery. Those things are from Satan, designed to keep us bound. Today you may be looking at a big obstacle blocking your way. If you are, it's time to do something about it. Weeping at the foot of the obstacle won't move it, and talking about how bad it is won't make it go away any quicker.

You can use the Word of God to help you. The Word is powerful enough to miraculously heal your hurts and the mountains in your life. All you've got to

 *Epilogue*

do is believe it! Once you do, then you can be on top of what was designed to hold you back. Remember that you can't have a testimony until you have a test! That's the part none of us want but it's what testimonies are made of! You've got an opportunity to use your faith and trample on the devil! Spend time with God and let His glory come out of your inner man like lightning. Let it consume your life.

You choose what you are going to do – nobody but you. Deuteronomy 30:18 says, *"...I have set before you life and death, the blessing and the curse. So choose life..."* Romans 6:23 tells us, *"the wages of sin is death."* When we choose to sin or do anything that is outside of God's will for our life we have chosen death. Does that mean physical death? Sometimes but, it also means death to joy, peace, happiness, prosperity and anything and everything in between. Sin destroys these areas of our life. These things may be hard to hear but, it's the truth and if you'll take your mind off that problem in your life and fill it with the Spirit of God, read His word, find a church that will teach you the fullness of God's Word and not water it down, you will make it.

Once you do these things, you'll find that you can't help but sit on top of your problem as an overcomer and victoriously proclaim what the Lord has done for you! Isaiah 45:2 says, *"I will go before thee, and make the crooked places straight: I will break in pieces the gates of brass, and cut asunder the bars of iron."*

Anchored In His Love

Many people say that God's going to make the straight places crooked but, that's a lie. They don't know God, they know of Him but they obviously don't *know* Him. Some of you are tied up in divorce problems, marital problems, financial problems, homosexuality, and alcoholism, and someone has told you that God is trying to teach you something. It's a lie! Would you stick your child's hand in the fire to teach him that fire burns! *Absolutely not.* If someone is telling you that God killed your baby, it's a lie! God created that baby and wanted him or her to grow in the knowledge of who He is. God doesn't kill people and He didn't kill my brother.

How do I know that! Because the Bible says in John 10:10 that it is the *devil who comes to steal, kill and destroy.* In that same scripture it tells us that Jesus came to give life and give it more abundantly! Talk to Jesus...He loves you. Jesus will move the mountains that have come against you. He said that we would have trials on this earth but He would walk through the situation with us. YOU are never alone.... did you hear me, YOU are *never* alone. So, start today, start now. Use every obstacle as a stepping stone or pulpit to proclaim the Good News to everyone that God sends your way and maybe next time I will be reading your book. Hallelujah!!!

To GOD be the Glory. Amen!

www.ingramcontent.com/pod-product-compliance
Lightning Source LLC
Chambersburg PA
CBHW051437290426
44109CB00016B/1598